AF425717

A
R
D
WRITING WITH YOU
IN MIND

Shanna Coles' life changed the moment she heard her son's name and saw his face flash across her television as a wanted fugitive. Shanna watched in horror and pain while her son was arrested and thrown into a police car on the six o'clock news.

She almost lost her sanity, her family and her will to live because she didn't understand.

HOW SHE RAISED A MURDERER!!

Shanna will relive some painful moments of her life that will lead her to the breakthrough she has been searching for.

Written by: **Antoinette R. Davis**

This book is a work of fiction. Any references to historical events, real people, or real places are used fictitiously. Other characters, names, places, and events are products of the author's imagination and any resemblance to actual events or places or persons living or deceased is entirely coincidental.

For more information, contact:

Antoinettewrites@aol.com

www.1fictionqueen.com

ONLY child, publishing

CHAPTER ONE

The End

We had big dreams and plans for our son when he was born, I dreamed of him playing in the NFL, becoming a lawyer, a doctor, or joining the military like his grandfather. I certainly never planned on this, (tears) my son is gone and I'm here packing his clothes to give away. I was overwhelmed with emotions; I sat down on my son's bed and recalled. "I wanted more for you," I couldn't stop the tears, "I'm sorry we failed you son."

An hour later, I was nervous as I prepared myself for what would be one of the worst days of my life. I had barely eaten over the last few months or done anything for myself, or my other children, and I didn't want to show my face at work or on the streets. I wore shame like a designer suit. Everywhere I went people recognized me, pointed fingers, and whispered around me. I was hanging on to my job with a thread and my family members talked about me but not with me and it was the same with friends.

I walked into the courtroom alone and was noticed immediately by everyone, I felt like I was on trial, and truthfully I was. Everything I had done from the time Wendell was born was on trial, in the media, and in the courtroom.

The judge called Wendell's name, and he and his attorney stood up, and my heart sank, I held my chest and lowered my head, and said a prayer.

The judge read the charges.

"Wendell Stewart Jr. you are charged with First-degree murder, possession of a deadly weapon, and carjacking. The jury found you guilty," Judge Anderson adjusted his glasses, sipped his water, and cleared his throat; meanwhile, I was on the edge of my seat. The judge leaned forward; I could see the sweat on his forehead from across the room. "Young man I am sentencing you to LIFE without the possibility of parole."

A cry rang out, I looked over to my left and it was Loraine, Sabian's mother crying. I could only imagine that she was crying because she was happy and felt justice was served but my inner cry was pain. I dared not cry out loud, for what, my son was a murderer.

The judge asked Sabian's family to come and read a victim impact statement.

Loraine walked to the front of the courtroom with her husband Gill and their other children. I knew Gill from around the neighborhood, his mother was Wendell's daycare provider while I worked two sometimes three jobs.

As Loraine started to speak I could hear the pain in her voice. "My son was a good person; from the time he was a little boy, I knew he would be great. He was always reading and he loved to learn. My family was overjoyed when he was accepted into college on a scholarship. He got a job at Walmart for the summer so he could have money to take with him when he left for college and, my family and I never thought anything would happen to him." Tears streamed from all of their faces and Sabian's sister hugged her mother to comfort her. Sabian's mother pointed at Wendell, "YOU, YOU NASTY VILE HUMAN TOOK MY SON'S LIFE FOR NOTHING, HE DIDN'T HAVE ANY MONEY ON HIM AND YOU KILLED HIM FOR THAT!" Her voice was booming and her anger was felt throughout the courtroom. "I DON'T CARE HOW YOU WERE RAISED; YOU DIDN'T HAVE THE RIGHT TO TAKE MY SON'S LIFE, IT WAS NOT YOUR LIFE TO TAKE. HE WAS MY CHILD,"

At this point I'm crying, I'm a mother after all and I felt her pain.

"I HOPE YOU ROT IN A JAIL CELL AND LIVE LIKE AN ANIMAL IN HELL, ALONG WITH YOUR FAMILY!"

I looked up at her and her eyes were fixed on me.

I felt like I deserved her anger because my childhood pain and trauma set Wendell's downfall in motion.

Wendell stood up in the courtroom handcuffed and shackled around his ankles. He looked up and his squinted eyes glanced around the courtroom, he was looking for me, not anyone else, not his father, grandparents, or siblings, just me. I had always been there for him. Our eyes met just as he was being led out of the courtroom, and I stared at him the same way I did when I first saw him as a baby in the nursery. He was my first-born child, and precious. He was born perfect, with beautiful dark complex skin, and dimples that put a smile on everyone's face. I lost my son to the streets, gangs, and self-hatred.

I wanted to sneak out of the courtroom unnoticed, so I put on sunglasses and a hat. I was tired of the news media ripping me apart and telling the world I was a bad mother. Unfortunately, I wasn't successful at laying low as soon as I stepped onto the pavement the reporters ran toward me.

 "Ms. Cole, do you think your son got a fair trial," one reporter asked.

I moved quickly toward the parking garage, but not quick enough because soon I was swarmed with reporters.

"Ms. Cole, what would you like to say to the family of Sabian Knight," a reporter asked?

I stopped I felt compelled to answer the reporter's question, for months I wanted to say something to Sabian's family but I didn't know just what to say and now I was put on the spot.

I started to speak but nothing came out, I was at a loss for words just as I had been for months. I looked into the camera, and I felt the warm tears rolling down my cheeks, I shook my head and walked away, I knew that anything I said would be held against me. The news media had already exploited me. Thank goodness they didn't follow me to my car.

I sat in my car in the parking garage that faced the city central prison and I cried it out, I kept hitting the steering wheel and I yelled and screamed, "Why Wendell, why did you destroy your life, why would do this, why, why!"

I asked him over and over during the trial why, the judge asked, the lawyers asked him and he never gave a reason as to why he killed an innocent fifteen-year-old young black man.

I needed to pull myself together so I could go to work, I had missed a lot of time from work in the past year going back and forth to court, visiting lawyers, and the prison. I was lucky to still have a job.

I arrived at work late, and on my way to my office I spoke, but no one spoke back. I closed my office door, sat down, and attempted to get some work done, but I knew I wasn't going to get much done because my mind was on Wendell.   I kept trying to focus; minutes later my supervisor called me into her office. I was nervous, I was already skating on thin ice. "But I can't be fired can I?" I thought to myself.

I gathered what little nerves I had left and walked over to her office. I was surprised to see the director of Capital One Bank along with the CEO.

"Close the door please,"

"I thought to myself, "This can't be good." I sat down in front of them, took a deep breath, and braced myself. Anytime I saw white men in suites, I knew it was going to be some bullshit.

Miss Myers pulled out a folder, "Your work over the past year has not met our company standards, and I'm afraid we're going to have to let you go."

"Just like that, no warning, no writeups," I'm saying to myself.

"Okay, I get it, they are using the black woman to take me down while their snow possum asses watch, okay," I said to myself.

"Does this have anything to do with my son being convicted of murder?"

The CEO coughed and cleared his throat and the director looked at Ms. Myers. I guess they wanted the house nigga to answer.

Ms. Myers looked at me as if to say, "Girl, you know it is, stop."

But I wanted to hear what she had to say.

"This has to do with your performance, Shanna."

I nodded my head and stood up, "Okay I'll clean out my desk."

"No need, I'll have that done and we will send you your things," says Ms. Myers.

I walked out of her office and walked into my old office, grabbed my jacket, and walked out, I was so mad, I could have let the place up with a semi-automatic. But what good would that have done? By the time I got to the elevator, I saw security standing there waiting. I guess they were there for me.

I lost my son, and now my job the only thing left is to lose me. I worked so hard not to be like them, I wanted to be better than my drugged-up, drunken ass parents.

Right now, a crack pipe, a drink, and some pills would take all my pain away so I thought.

CHAPTER TWO

The cause.

When I was a kid, my dad was everything. He was strong, a provider, believed in education, had money, took care of our family financially, protected us, always smelled good, wore suits, was smart as a whip, and never spared the Rod.

When my mom and dad divorced I was six years old, and I was devastated because I didn't understand what was really going on.

My sister, brother, and I moved with my mother and her boyfriend Ralph, and then my aunt Tammy and then finally we got our own home in Simons Garden. That house never felt like a home, but my mother tried to make it that way. It just felt temporary.

One day my sister and I went to my dad's house with his new girlfriend Joann and her children Dawn and Bobby. Joanne had another daughter Desiree but she lived with her dad. That should have been a sign there but it wasn't.

One day my mom called my dad while we were there for the weekend and we eavesdropped on the conversation. My mom said how about we do one year on and one year off.

He agreed to it and shortly after that, our lives changed forever.

It was cool over at my dad's house because his house was better than the one my mom tried to have for us. Besides my mom was struggling to take care of us and my father had the means to provide a better life for us.

It was supposed to be for only a year, I didn't have a sense of time but it couldn't be that long, I remember thinking to myself. What can go wrong, we were with our dad.

Things were good until they weren't. My dad and JoAnn would go to work and hang out. While they were gone, JoAnn's children would torment us, and Desiree was the worst.

Even though I was the youngest, I would tell them to beat me more so my sister wouldn't get hurt so much. I loved her and besides, she was a little timider than I was.

They beat us every single day for a whole summer and that is no exaggeration. I remember one time I got fed up and tried to fight back. Got my ass whooped but I was tired of it.

Finally, my dad and Ms. JoAnn broke up, that was the best news ever for us. He kicked her and her children out of our house and things were okay for a split second. Hell has no fury like a woman's scorn, well that was true because Ms. JoAnn turned off our gas and electricity. It was in her name.

My dad literally had to cook for us on top of a kerosene heater. He was so resilient and made shit happen.

He continued going to work, looking good and smelling good even in a house with no electricity. I didn't care about electricity; I had my dad and that's all I cared about.

I was sure the one year was up but we were still staying at our dad's house. My mom dropped by every now and then to see us. I remember her coming over one Christmas, she took us to her tiny apartment, gave us toys and then she vanished into thin air.

One year turned into two and three and it was just me, my siblings, and my dad. We were a family.

This is not my dad.

My dad got a girlfriend, Dorothea, she was skinny, dark-skinned, and ugly. She looked like she came from the wrong side of the railroad tracks. I felt it in my spirit that she was going to be bad news and I was right. I might have been young but I was wise enough to know that she was not good for my dad.

She had a missing tooth, as handsome as my father was, what did he possibly see in her, I wondered. It was like my dad gave up.

 She started off really nice and sweet, she would take me and my sister out with her when she went to the projects to visit family and friends. We didn't know what the projects were but it didn't take us long to figure it out.

Things were changing with my dad, he was starting to smoke cigarettes, and once he lost his job; he was moving differently and by that I mean he was doing some weird shit. Seeing him with a cigarette didn't become him at all.

The house we were in started falling apart. There were roaches everywhere, the electricity was on and off, no running water at times, and the refrigerator was broken.

We did have a floor-model tv and VCR. I remember coming home one day from school early and was at the top of the stairs when I heard a noise. I saw my dad and Dorothea dressed in black and taking the VCR and other small things out of the house. Then later that day they acted as if we were robbed, but I saw them. Like WTF, are we really doing this huh? Okay

My dad became very abusive physically. I remember one summer I got my ass beat every single day. He would beat me with a weight belt, his fists, and anything else he got his hands on.

One day Dorothea was on the couch. I looked at her dead in her face and said, "I am going to kill you". I meant it with every ounce of my being. Of course, the punk bitch told my dad and he beat me. He punched me dead up in my nose, and blood was everywhere. He never asked me why I said that to her, he just took her side.

I wanted to kill her because she stole my dad from me and turned him into a monster.

The monster

My sister and I were eating off of burnt spoons, that's
when we had food because most of the time, we didn't
have food. Strange men and women were in our house
all the time, day, and night. I later found out they were
there to get high. We never had food in the house and
he would leave us for days at a time by ourselves with
no electricity sometimes.
However, we still got up and went to school every
day. I was teased a lot in school because I smelled and
I looked horrible. I couldn't take a bath, there was no
one to wash our clothes or do our hair. My hair fell out
terribly. I rocked a little Jerri curl but that went to shit
once that bitch came into our lives. My dad would put
the pink moisture in my hair and comb me a bang and
slick the back. It was hideous but I'd didn't
care. Why, because my dad did my hair.
But…..
He became so much of a monster; he started giving my
twelve-year-old brother crack and they would get high
together. All this was happening right above our heads
in his room or down in the basement. My sister and I
always stayed in the living room. We had no cable so
we could only watch VCR tapes. My favorite was the
golden child with Eddie Murphy. I would sit in front
of the tv late at night watching it over and over. Well,
at least until they sold the VCR for crack.
I remember one day my dad was off his freaking
rockers, he came downstairs and gave my sister and
me a book of 65.00 food stamps a piece. Now mind
you we never knew what this paper money in a book

was before meeting Dorothea but we knew we could
buy food with it.
We lived on 35th Street and the store we went to was
on 30th and Jefferson. It was black-owned at that
time. Mind you my sister and I hadn't eaten in a few
days so I said to her, "I'm gonna get me everything I
can get." I didn't know how to count food stamps
because in my mind it was different than money,
I walked up in that store and let me tell you, I brought
every canned good fruit, soup, bread, candy, and
drink. We had no refrigerator and we couldn't cook so
I had to get stuff I could just eat from the can.
My sister says, "I'm going get something now but save
the rest of my money".

I said, "Shiiitt! I'm spending all of mine."
When I left out of there all of my paper money was
spent. When we got back home we were met by
Delaware's finest junkies in our basement.
I plopped my ass on the floor in front of the floor
model tv, put on The Golden Child, and opened my
can of pears. Got me a burnt spoon and went to town.
My sister was behind me eating whatever.

My dad came up from that basement and geeked the
fuck out!!! He went to my sister first and said, "Where
are those books of food stamps at? She started crying
and gave him all that she didn't spend and then he
looked at me and said, "Shae Shae how much do you
have left?"

I looked him in his face, and before I tell you what I
said. Picture my frail ass, black, bald-headed because

these fools ain't maintenance my curl and now all my hair has fallen out, big rabbit teeth with gaps, and thick eyebrows.

I looked at my dad in his face and said with a sinister grin, "I spent all of it." I turned back to the tv and continued watching the movie as if he wasn't standing there.

That nigga slapped the living fuck outta me, but I didn't give two shits because I was full and I had more food stashed.

I felt bad for my sister though. She really was trying to save what she had, but he took it. I shared my food with my sister, but that was just one night of many horrors."

"Shana, I'm afraid our hour is up, can you come back next week?"

"I don't know, I don't have a job now, how am I supposed to pay you?"

"Don't worry about that, you just come back next week."

"Okay, next week."

CHAPTER THREE

Therapy lasted longer than I had anticipated and I know Everyone says, "Get therapy" but what they don't tell me is reliving that shit is hard. I fight with my thoughts every day to forget my shitty childhood if I can even call it a childhood. Every time I left my therapist's office I felt drained, but if I want to get to the root of my problems.

It's raining like crazy out here, I better pull over, I hate the rain. I better call home and let the sitter know I'm going to be a little later.

"Hello," a man answers the phone.

"Hello, I'm sorry I dialed the wrong number."

"No you didn't dial the wrong number, it's me your ex, Gary."

"What, what are you doing in my house!"

"I came to spend some time with my children and…… to see you."

I was annoyed and angry, he knew I didn't want to see him. "Where is Gary Jr.

"I'm on my home right now!" I hung up on him. I knew he wanted some money, that's why he dropped by.

I drove over the speed limit so I could catch every green light; my black BMW was zooming in and out of traffic and I didn't care about the pouring rain.

I'm going to take this red light; I hope I make it.

Her light changed to red and a car on the opposite side took off immediately at his green light. Shana and the car hit.

My car came to a screeching halt, this is all I need for an accident to happen and my insurance will go up.

A short white man got out of his car, looked at the damage, and then walked up to my car. "Ms., you ran the light and hit my car!"

I wanted to say something smart but I was too defeated, "Look I'm sorry, I was in a rush to get home."

"I don't care about that girl."

"Wait a minute, did this white person just call me a girl?' I got out of my car so he could see I was not a girl.

I got out and walked around to the front and side of my car to see the damage. Oh no, my car is messed up.

"You see, you see what you did."

Is he pointing his finger at me, yes he is? I looked around to see who had stopped and what do you know here comes the police. The white man runs up to the officer.

"Sir she ran the light and hit my car."

The police walked over to me."

"ma'am is that what happened?"

Right away I thank God he is a black cop and a handsome black cop at that.

"Yes officer, I didn't see the light had turned red."

"Were you on your phone?"

"No sir, I was not."

"Check her she looks like she's been drinking."

"Little white man shut the fuck up," I screamed in my head and then I look back at the officer. "I haven't been drinking, but I had a bad day, maybe the worst day of my life. I lost my job, my son." I stopped; I didn't want to say anything else.

"I'm sorry to hear that but I'm going to have to give you a ticket for running the light."

"I understand, officer," I'm trying to be charming.

"I need your insurance card and registration."

I walked back to my car, soaking wet from the rain; I got my registration and insurance card and handed them to the officer. I'm shaking cold but I'm really shaking because my insurance card is outdated.

"Ma'am, your insurance is canceled."

I immediately got a lump in my throat.

"I told you; you people never have insurance."

I was pissed and I hoped the black officer was too, I looked at him as if to say, "Check him."

"Sir, get back in your car and wait for me."

The little white man snubbed both of us.

"Ms. Cole, you are driving with no insurance, I can have your car towed."

"No, no, no, officer I promise I will have insurance tomorrow." I started crying, I couldn't control myself. My whole day had finally hit me, I threw myself into his broad chest and cried all my pain and frustration away. His big strong arms held me like I needed to be held.

"Okay, I'll let you go with a ticket but you need to get insurance asap."

He felt sorry for me, thank God. I lifted my head off of him and looked up into his face. I felt like a damsel in distress but I was really a mess and suddenly I remembered Gary was in my house and I needed to get home. "Thank you, officer, you don't know how much I appreciate this."

As I was driving away I looked in my rearview mirror at the officer standing tall and sexy in his uniform. Shit, I haven't been with a man in years, Wendell and his in and out of trouble kept me busy mentally and physically.

I pulled up and saw Gary's car in my driveway where I'm supposed to park my car, damn him.

Amanda greets me at the door, Mommy, Mommy, you're home."

"Yes, mommy is home, where is your father?"

"He went upstairs to use the bathroom."

"I'll be right back," I didn't care that I was dripping water on my hardwood floors, I needed to find Gary fast. I eased up the stairs and there he was in my bedroom, looking through my shit. He didn't even hear me pull up outside, so busy looking for shit. I stood behind him with my arms crossed. I could smell the weed on him.

I was calm, "What are you looking for?"

"Oh, oh hey Shana, baby, I was looking for a band-aid."

"Bull shit, you were looking for money or jewelry, get the fuck out of my house, now!"

"Shhhh, lower your voice, you don't want Amanda to hear you."

I took a deep breath because I know I can go to one hundred and kill this man. "Leave, please and don't come back when I'm not here."

"You're crazy, this used to be my house and my children live here. I can see my children."

"The only time you want to see either of them is when you want something."

"Why are you wet, your clothes and hair, you look a mess."

"How the hell am I supposed to look, my oldest son just got life in prison for murder. I thought you were coming to court with me today."

"I had to work; they wouldn't let me off."

He is lying, "he's not your son, so I didn't expect you to support me."

"Hold up that's mean."

I yanked my arm away from him, "Get off me, don't touch me."

"Daddy, come on, you said you were going to play a game with me."

"He's coming, but he can't stay."

"Go down there and tell her you can't stay."

"Nope, I'm staying I want to spend time with her and I miss my family."

This is straight bull shit coming from him, "I want you to leave right now, or I'm calling the police and having you removed."

"Shana I need some money, and I know you have some for a rainy day. Just let me hold a few dollars and when I get back on my feet I'll bring it back."

"Dad, come on!"

"I'm going downstairs and play a few games with her and then I'll leave I promise."

I let him walk in front of me, I wanted to search him to see if he had taken anything, but I knew he would never find anything. I learned to hide my money from him years ago.

"By the way, why don't you fix us some dinner while we play the game?"

"No, I'm going to order me and my family some dinner and help Amanda with her homework."

"I did that already, baby, I got this, relax and I'll take a cheesesteak sub with everything."

I feel an anxiety attack coming on, this happens whenever I don't express my true feelings when I'm angry. "Gary, get the hell out of my house and stay out."

"Mommy, what's wrong." Amanda starts crying.

"Go upstairs and wait for me, now!"

"Don't yell at her because you're having a bad day."

I'm not just having a bad day, I am having a bad life, but I needed to calm down before I kill him. "Gary I don't have any money to give you, I have to take care of these kids and this house."

"If you let me move back in I can help you with all of that."

Is he joking, nope he's not. "Fool I'm not helping you. My days of helping you are over! Leave now!"

"You crazy bitch, I hope you lose all of this shit, and don't call me when your black ass is sitting on the street."

There he is, that's the motherfucker I know, the selfish, mean-ass.

Amanda yells from upstairs, "Daddy, you're leaving!"

"Yes, your mother is crazy."

I slammed the door when he walked out of it, thank God he is gone. Now for the hard part explaining to our daughter why her father isn't allowed in this house when I'm not home.

I walked up to her bedroom, and she looked at me mad. I'm always the bad guy.

I sat down next to her, "Let's talk, I know you are confused, and I'm sorry about that. Your father has not been a responsible person, do you know what that means?"

She shook her head, "he didn't clean his room."

I had to laugh, "No not his room, but he didn't clean up his life, it's a mess, stuff thrown all over the place, and until he is responsible enough to clean up his life we, meaning, you, your brother and I can't be around him."

"Is Wendell coming home," She asked looking hopeful, "I pray for him every night."

I closed my eyes, and tears started swelling in my eyes, but I held them back, "No baby, your brother isn't coming home for a long time."

I watched the tears fall from her beautiful innocent eyes, "do you want a hug?"

"Yes, but you're wet, why are you so wet?"

"That's another story for another day, but how about I get changed, order us some food and we go downstairs and play a game and wait for Gary Jr. to come home from football practice.

She smiled and showed me her snagger tooth mouth, I was happy to get a smile. "Okay, I bet you can't beat me."

"Well, we'll have to see about that."

I could wait to wash the day I had off of me, but all the soap in the world can't wash the thoughts of my son spending the rest of his life behind bars. The baby I held in my arms and helped take his first steps.

They say your firstborn child gets all of your mistakes and having him at fifteen years old, I definitely made some mistakes.

I stepped out of the shower and saw my phone blinking I had a missed call, "Who is this?" I called the number back.

"Hello, Ms. Cole."

"Yes, this is Ms. Cole."

"This is Officer Brown; I was calling to make sure you got home safe."

"Yes, I'm home, that's nice of you to check on me."

"No problem ma'am have a good night."

I thought that was nice of him and I had better get some insurance soon before Officer Brown handcuffed me and I didn't need that.

A week later, a therapy session

I walked into my therapist's office feeling worse than I did last week and I haven't been able to sleep because of Wendell. Last night I got a call from some man telling me Wendell was on lockup for fighting another inmate over a can of tuna.

"Have a seat, Shana, I love your outfit, you look nice."

I couldn't break a smile, "Thank you, I wish I felt like my outfit looked."

"So first thing, I'm glad you decided to keep your appointment. How are things?"

"Things are okay, I found a job and it pays well, it's paying more than I was making and I decided to go into business for myself?"

"That's nice, I am impressed, what type of business?"

Business Accounting, I am launching my website next month, right in time for tax season."

"Good for you, sounds like you are going to be very busy."

I took a deep breath because she is right I am going to be very busy, "That's how I cope with life by staying busy."

"Make yourself comfortable and tell me what's on your mind today."

"I was fearful of my dad, that man did not spare the rod or his fists; I loved him so much but I was scared of him too!!!! Prime example, I was always missing the bus and I mean always, so I could understand his frustration when he had to take me to school because of my carelessness.
Well one day, he said, Shana, if you miss the bus one more time, I'm gonna kick your ass.
One day I was running late for school and I heard the kids say, "The bus!!!!"
I darted out of the house so fast and crossed our street to chase the bus but never made it. A car driving up 35th Street fast hit me and I landed in the next block. I was scared but all I could think about was catching the bus so my father wouldn't beat the shit out of me
When I caught the bus at the next stop I was messed up, with scratches and bruises everywhere. I looked so disheveled. But I didn't care, I leaned my head against the window and looked at my house as we pulled off. I knew I didn't have to get my ass whooped by that man that day!!!
When word got out I got hit by a car, the police called my dad and he had to leave work to come to school. I spoke to the police and gave them the description of the car and as soon as the police left my father looked at me with his lips tight and whispered in my ear, "Why the fuck did you get up." I looked at my dad all confused, ugly, and bruised, and said "You told me if I miss the bus one more time you were going to beat me". He looked at me and said, "You so stupid, we could have gotten money for them hitting you". Well

damn, I couldn't win for losing.
I always wanted to please my dad but I couldn't
however my sister was the good child and she got all
the attention. She was smart and cute and despite our
challenges with wearing dirty clothes and no running
water, she managed to carry herself well. I on the
other hand showed all the signs of abuse that went
unnoticed in school. Teachers never asked why I
smelled so bad, why I wore clothes that had stains on
them, why this child's hair has long pieces and short
pieces, why this child's hair is not combed, and why is
she always on a damn diet! Yeah, that's what I used to
say at lunchtime because my dad didn't put any money
in our account or his checks kept bouncing. You see,
he was too proud to get us a free lunch but he had no
money to get us lunch. I'm still confused by that!
I was skinny and frail. I really looked like the starving
kids in the commercials back in the 80s. The only
thing I didn't have was flies on my eyelids, however,
all signs of starvation were there. Skinny with a big
ole stomach and none of the adults in the school said
anything, but the students said a lot. They roasted me
every day and all day; bullying was to the extreme but
nobody wanted to fight me. Hell, I wouldn't have
either, I mean think about it, you never fight the kid
who looks like they're struggling because they will
fight to the death and I would. The mean things they
said to me and about me, caused me to be mean, on top
of how my dad treated me. I built this wall up so the
words couldn't hurt me. I knew I couldn't change my
lifestyle, so I made myself smart. Not book smart, but

smart in the sense that I just soaked everything up and learned. I was good in school with minimum studying. Hell, I couldn't study back then, our lights barely worked. I knew I had to throw myself into something because my home life was so bad. I thought if I got good grades my dad would come home but nope he left my sister and me in a cold house during the winter and a hot house during the summer alone with no one to take care of us.

I recall Christmas with my dad, we always had a real tree up and it would be the biggest and ugliest tree standing in the corner of his house. I mean the decoration was the ugliest however, every year we could count on a tree in the house. One Christmas my dad did not bring home a tree until the night before Christmas and we didn't have any decorations so my sister and I tried to take household stuff to decorate the tree. My brother saw there was absolutely nothing under the tree and he went out and got us all types of stuff. He brought us back robes, night clothes, and toys. My mom stopped by and dropped us off our bikes, she didn't come in, she just left them at the door. We were happy, that is until my dad and his ugly girlfriend stole it all and sold it for crack. It was a typical life at this point and this is where I believe I developed selfishness and jealousy. I mean honestly, everything we got was taken from us, other kids had everything I needed. Damn, the wants!!! Everything I needed, like matching socks, hell socks that didn't have hard dirt on them and they would get soft again as you wore them, a refrigerator, no roaches, food,

running water, electricity. I mean damn!!! I remember I would be on the bus and look at the houses that were decorated for the holidays. I used to say, "My house is gonna look just like that! I'm going to decorate just like those white people on Shipley Road and I'm gonna live in one of those houses my kids will be happy to come home to."
You know, despite all the trauma and drama I experienced with my dad. I still remember this one incident. One day he went out to buy his drugs and on our way back home he stopped at a gas station to go to the bathroom. There was a white man with big square glasses on his face parked next to us. My sister and sat in the car waiting for our dad and I saw my dad touch the bathroom door and look behind him. Next thing you know, my dad comes running back to the car and looked back and me and my sister and said. Did y'all hear him? My sister and I looked and said no. My dad said, "That man said if I go into the bathroom. Y'all won't be here when I get out."   I don't know if it happened or he was geeking from the drugs but in my eyes, my dad loved me because he could have gone in that bathroom or he could have pimped me and my sister when he didn't have any drugs but he never did and that is why I had respect for him. He protected me and my sister that day and despite all the horrible stuff he had done before that day, I held on to that particular incident. I was getting older and I said enough is enough, I have got to get us out of here even though I was still holding onto "My dad has to love me, number 1 I was his child, and number two he saved us from

being raped or killed. However, things were taking a toll for the worse, the roaches were getting worse and we were going on years and bitch ass Dorothea was still there, he was still getting high, clothes still not getting washed, the refrigerator still not working, and shit is not getting better.

I wrote a letter in school and gave it to Ms. Cusanelli my 4th-grade teacher at PS Dupont. I asked her to mail this letter to my pop pop. I don't know if she read the letter but if she did, the cops would have been knocking on the door, but they never did. Which meant she didn't read or didn't care. Or she read it and thought whoever I was writing this letter to needed to come to get us asap. With much anticipation and anxiety, I waited and hoped my pop pop got the letter. I don't know if weeks or a month or so later, my pop pop showed up at that house!!! My sister and I were about to be saved. We sat at the top of the stairs and heard my dad and Pop-pop talking. My dad wouldn't let my pop pop past the entryway of the covered porch. He didn't want him to see how bad the house looked, I guess. Hell, it wasn't anything in there but a couch at that point. Anyway, pop pop was there to take us away from the hell our father had us in. Next thing I know we didn't hear pop pop's voice anymore. Our dad had lied to him and told him everything was fine and he wouldn't allow him to see us. I wanted to run down the stairs to my pop pop but my father would have killed me on the spot.

I kept saying over and over, "We are dead," I knew it was about to go down, he was going to kill us.

My dad yelled at us to come downstairs and we ran down the stairs faster than a speeding bullet and I am not lying to you. He slid my body clear across the kitchen floor and needless to say, I don't remember anything after that.

There was another time my dad got on us about cleaning, and so we both went into the kitchen to clean it and this is when I saw my sister had some true gangster in her. She took the can of roach spray and sprayed the cereal boxes, and my father ate cereal every day sometimes all day.

He got his favorite bowl of Corn Pops and his mouth immediately started burning.

He picked up the box to see what was wrong and it was roach spray all at the bottom of the box. My sister took one to the head that day because he beat her with a shoe, the heel part.

That man wasn't my dad, that man was an addict and he wasn't in his right mind. I started making excuses for his behavior. As time progressed I just knew it would change and he would get better but it wasn't happening fast enough for me. I gave up on my mom coming to get us because we had been living in hell for five years and she apparently didn't give a damn. He was draining the life out of me."

I saw Dr. Parker look at her watch, my time must be up. Thank God, I'm drained.

"Shana, we're going to stop, our time is up but I definitely want to see you next week."

I noticed my therapist had taken off her glasses and her eyes were red, "Why next week, why can't I come once a month."

"Right now, we need to see each other every week, and I'm going to write you a prescription for something to help you relax, you need to get sleep and rest."

I chuckled, "Sleep, how am I supposed to sleep when my son is in prison?"

"Did you sleep when he was on the street and in trouble?"

"No, I didn't, how could I when I knew he was self-destructing."

"When do you rest, Shana?"

I'll rest when I'm dead, I thought to myself, "I don't rest, my mind doesn't allow me that opportunity."

I looked over at Dr. Parker and she wrote me a prescription.

"Here, get this filled and see if that helps."

I took the paper but I didn't want to, "Dr. Parker, I have never taken medication and I don't plan on starting."

"This will help you."

I took the prescription but I have no plans on taking the medication.

I walked out to my car, the sun had gone down and it was dark, but when I looked up I didn't see any stars. I remember when I was a little girl I used to wish upon a star. Silly of me, that was a fantasy, because nothing changed.

CHAPTER FOUR

Life must go on.

I spent the next two weeks setting up my new office. I ordered a desk and a new computer from Walmart. I wanted everything to be new well almost everything, so I went to a secondhand store and purchased a chair. I was so excited about my new business that I didn't have time to sleep. I was spending my days and nights dreaming about my new business and I'm sure Bill Gates and Jay-z never slept. I am so sure this is going to work, actually, it has to work because I turned down the new job offer and took my 401k money out so I could have a cushion. The crazy part is if Gary would pay child support it would be a big help, but that's wishful thinking, he only thinks about himself. I looked around the basement and smiled; it came together nicely.

I spent two weeks driving around to salons and barbershops in the neighborhood and introducing myself and handing out flyers and my business card. I could have called around but I wanted to introduce myself and I needed to pitch what I could offer them.

My cell phone wasn't ringing for business; however, Wendell was ringing my phone all day. I listened to him complain about prison, I told him I loved him, and he talked to his sister and brother. Gary Jr. didn't want to talk to him at all. I had to make him get on the phone. Gary Jr. was hurt, disappointed, and tired of getting teased at school. In his mind, his big brother and best friend were gone and were never coming back.

I started getting in my head, what if this doesn't work. I didn't have room for tears only the hustle.

It's been a couple of weeks and I haven't gotten a text, email, or phone call and I passed out over two hundred flyers and business cards. Why aren't they calling me, I know they need an accountant, but I'm in my head with doubt.

I started dinner because Amanda and Gary Jr. would be home soon and I wanted them to have a home-cooked meal at least once a week.

My cell phone rung, I ran to get it from my purse, "Hello,"

"Hello, Ms. Cole?"

"Yes, this is Ms. Cole.

"I'm calling from the Sheriff's department."

Oh, God, I grabbed my chest, what is wrong. "Why are you calling me."

"Your son escaped custody and we believe he is coming to you."

Just as he said that there was a knock on the door, I panicked.

"We are sending the police to your house just in case he shows up there, they should be arriving now."

"Hold on someone is at the door," I opened the door and saw a big white man staring down at me and a swat team on my manicured lawn and in the street.

"Ma'am, may I come in?"

I was speechless, I just opened the door to let him in, and immediately he started looking around with his eyes.

I shook my head, "He is not here."

Amanda's school bus pulled up, I hung up the phone and ran to the door and the police officer grabbed my arm.

"Get your hands off of me!"

"Ma'am I can't let you leave the house."

I yanked my arm from him, "My daughter's school bus just pulled up and I don't want her to be afraid when she gets off the bus; I need to go and get her!"

I walked out to the school bus with a fake smile, everyone on the block was standing outside and looking toward my house, "shit" I thought to myself. "Hey baby, how was your day?"

"Mommy why are these cops here, what's going on, I'm scared."

"Look at me, I am right here and you have no reason to be afraid. The police are here to protect us." We walked into the house.

Amanda put her books down and went to her room, I heard her scream.

I ran up to her room and saw her shaking, and pee was running down her leg, "what's wrong!"

She pointed to the two police officers searching her room, "Them, they are going to kill me like they did George Floyd and Briana Taylor."

I picked my baby up and took her to the bathroom, a police officer started following me and I snapped, "Get the fuck back, I'm taking my daughter to the bathroom, you have violated our privacy enough already."

"Ms., your son is a fugitive and a threat to the public, we have to make sure we protect the public."

I rolled my eyes at the officer and slammed the bathroom door and within minutes I heard Gary Jr.

"Ma, Ma, Momma!

He was screaming at the top of his lungs; I looked out of the bathroom window and saw the police had him on the ground. I told Amanda to lock the bathroom door behind me, and then I ran as fast as I could out the front door.

I started pushing the officer to get out of my way, "Get your motherfucking hands off of my son!"

"Ma," Gary Jr was crying his eyes out.

I stepped up to the cop, and grabbed my son, "Don't touch my son goddammit!"

"Who is he," asked the sheriff?

"He's not Wendell, he's my other son."

"We didn't know."

"Exactly my point, you think every black man looks alike!"

I looked at the two black cops out front, "What the fuck is your problem, you were going to let them kill him, you dumb motherfuckers." I walked Gary Jr into the house.

Gary Jr was panicking, "What is going on and why are they here, they attacked me when I started walking up to the door."

"Calm down and I'll explain, I need to get Amanda from the bathroom."

I cleaned Amanda up and brought her back downstairs to the living room. Gary Jr. was sitting on the couch still in shock, nothing like this had ever happened to him before.

I sat both of them down, "your brother escape from prison."

"What, he did what, why is he always ruining our lives, I hate him," says Gary Jr.

"I don't hate him, but he needs to stop doing bad things. I don't want the police to kill him," says Amanda.

My poor baby can't George Floyd and Brianna Taylor's murder out of her little mind. I should not have let her watch the news.

I couldn't look at either of them, "Yeah well, I don't either but it looks like that's a strong possibility," I thought to myself.

My cell phone rang, and I got up from the sofa to answer it, the police officer grabbed my phone before I could get it. "What are you doing!"

"Put the call on speaker, if it's Wendell, try to get a location, and do not tell him we are here."

I snatched my phone from the officer, "hello,"

"Hi, Ms. Cole my name is Valerie from House of Styles, you dropped off a flyer and a card.

"Yes, hello Valerie," I rolled my eyes at the officer and turned my back to him.

"The stylist in the salon would like to take your class on budgeting, retirement planning, and paying taxes. We can't stand on our feet forever," Valerie laughed.

"Oh that's great, go to my website and schedule the date and how many people will be attending." I was excited even if it was for a moment in time.

"Five stylists want to attend; do you have a group rate?"

"I do and it's on the website, everything you need is there and I do Zoom calls if someone wants to call in." I was smiling so hard.

I hung up and carried my phone with me.

The officer held out his hand, "I'll need to take that in case Wendell calls."

"No I'm not giving you my phone; this is my phone. You burst in here, scare my children and you're holding us hostage. You're not getting my phone."

The officer yells at me, "Ma'am this is serious, your son is a murderer and we don't know what he will do, he could kill innocent people again. Our job is to protect you and the citizens of Delaware, DO YOU UNDERSTAND THAT!"

Gary Jr. jumps up, "Don't yell at my mother, show her some respect!"

Wow, I looked at Gary Jr, my son was defending his mother, I was proud and scared for his life at the same time.

"I'm sorry, it's just that this is serious and we all want a good ending, we don't want anyone to get hurt."

"Including Wendell, right, you don't want him to get hurt either right?"

Gary Jr grabbed my hand, "Stop worrying about him, he picked his path now let him deal with the consequences!"

I wish it was that easy, how could he understand and how could I expect him to, Wendell made Gary Jr.'s life hard when he started getting into trouble. Wendell was jealous of Gary Jr. because he had his dad and his father was out on the street getting high.

I caressed his hand and shook my head, "I know you don't understand and I don't expect you to understand."

The three of us sat on the couch, all staring into space, but my mind was wandering.

The officer got a call over the radio, and my heart jumped, I tried to hear but they were talking in code.

"He carjacked an elderly man and his wife at a gas station and is headed East in a green Honda Accord."

My heart was racing, I know they are going to kill him, and for a split second, I felt guilty for what ran across my mind.

"Mommy, what's going on?"

Gary J jumped up, "Our brother is fucking up our lives again!"

He must be having a temporary moment of insanity, "Hey watch your mouth."

"Am I lying, you let him get away with everything and you take up for him. I'm tired of being his little brother. I hope they kill him!" He ran up to his room.

Amanda started crying, "No, no, don't say that I love Wendell, he's our brother."

I felt my heart beating through my chest, I wanted to break down and cry, my nerves were on edge just like when I was a little girl. Every time my father ran out of money to buy crack he would get mad at us and start yelling and beating us senselessly.

The police officer looked at me, he didn't feel anything for me as a mother, all he saw was a nigga, with a black son on the run.

Gary Jr.'s cell phone rang; the police heard it and ran up to his room and I ran behind them.

Gary Jr. reached into his bookbag for his phone and the police officer pointed his gun at him.

I lost it, "Put that shit away in my house and don't point it at my son, are you crazy. He's reaching for his phone!"

"Dad, come get me and Amanda, we're scared!"

"I want to speak to Daddy," says Amanda.

Gary Jr handed her the phone, "Daddy I'm scared too, the police made me pee on myself, I want to leave and stay with you."

I'm pacing the floor and keeping my eyes on the officer too.

Amanda hands me the phone, "Hello."

The officer looked at me, "Ma'am put the phone on speaker."

I didn't want to but I was tired of cussing my children weren't used to me talking like that. I put the phone on the speaker. "Gary I have you on speaker and an officer is starring down my throat."

"I heard about Wendell, it's bad Shana, he stole a car from a white elderly couple and their grandchild was in the car."

I don't remember much after that, just the room spinning, that's all I remember happening.
Two days later

I woke up and looked around, where was I? I couldn't focus my eyes, everything was blurry.

"Hello, you're finally woke."

The voice sounded familiar, I turned my head,

"Hey, you had us worried.

"Why, what happened?

"You are in the hospital."

"I'm in the hospital, why, what's wrong with me!"

"You passed out and you've been out for two days."

"Where are my children," I tried to lean up but I had IVs hooked to me.

"Relax, baby, they are with their dad at home."

Wait, I remember now, "Where is Wendell Jr.

My mother spoke softly, "He's still on the run."

I felt relieved, he was still alive.

I wanted to get up and leave, I didn't need to be here. I needed to be with my children.

My doctor, Dr. Taylor walked into the room, "How are feeling?"

Dr. Taylor thank God, someone I trust, "I feel fine and I want to go home and be with my children."

"I can't release you until your blood work comes back and we get an MRI on your brain and do an ultrasound on your heart."

I pleaded with her to release me but she didn't budge. I never like hospitals; I get anxious when I walk into a hospital.

"Dr. Taylor, I can make an appointment for those tests, let me leave the hospital."

Dr. Taylor could trust me, I took my health very seriously, and I could see in her expression that she wasn't going to release me.

"Shana, I can't release you yet, get these tests and once they come back, and if everything checks out we will release you."

Damn, I had her figured all wrong, "okay," I laid back on the bed and closed my eyes, I wanted to cry but once again, I couldn't, especially in front of my mother. She has never seen me be vulnerable and I sure as hell wasn't going to let her see it now.

I heard my cell phone ring; it was the ringtone I had for Gary J. "where is my phone?"

"Hey, ma are you going to be okay?"

I heard the fear in his voice, "Yes baby I'm going to be fine." I heard Amanda in the background "Let me speak to her."

"Mommy, I'm scared, you're going to die, are you going to die?"

"No, Mommy is not going to die, don't worry about me, I'll be home before you know it."

"Okay, I miss you, Daddy is here and he is cooking us some cool stuff to eat he took me to school yesterday and he walked me to my class and met my teachers."

Any little thing he does brings her joy, and her happiness was my happiness.

"I'm glad your dad is there to take care of you and your brother. Let me speak to your dad?"

"Hey baby, don't worry about anything, I am holding everything down just like I used to. Get better okay, Shana. I love you, girl."

I screamed in my head, thank God I'm in a hospital because he just made me sicker, if that's a word,

"Thanks, Gary. Have you heard anything about Wendell?"

My mother quickly spoke up, "I don't think you should worry about him right now."

I looked at her and rolled my eyes.

He hesitated so I knew something was wrong, "turn on the news, he all over the news, and Shana it's not good.

"What is it, just tell me!"

My mother placed her hand on my back and started rubbing my back, "Shana, calm down."

She never showed me affection as a child and now she wants to comfort me, "Gary, just tell me what's going on; I don't want to watch the news, they lie.

"Shana, he crashed the car he stole from the elderly couple and he beat and carjacked someone else."

"What about the couple's grandchild, what happened to him or her?"

"The child was in the car when he crashed it."

"Oh God, no."

"The police are still here at the house."

I closed my eyes; I couldn't believe my son was being hunted by the system like a runaway slave. It's a nightmare I would have never imagined for Wendell Jr.

"I know I wasn't the best husband and dad lately, but I'm going to be here for you and our children."

"Lately" I screamed in my head. He must think I lost my memory.

An hour later

The nurse came into my room and told me I had to go for X-rays and other tests.

"Shanna, I'm leaving, but I'll be back later, I have to go home and cook dinner for my husband."

She looked at me as if I wanted her to stay, "Okay."

As they were doing a sonogram on my heart, I was watching the monitor and I saw it beating. It was amazing to see my heart beating and pumping blood all through my body. I didn't think I had a whole heart because the people I love broke it piece by piece. It's funny how we say he or she broke my heart but mine was beating in one piece. I didn't know much about religion or God but at that moment I thought to myself, "Thank you God for protecting my heart."

After they rolled me back to my room, I stared at the ceiling, thinking about life. That's when I overheard two black nurses talking in the hallway right outside my room.

"You know that's his mother in that room, I hope they catch that monster and put his ass away for good."

"Girl, I was scared when I got off work last night, they are telling everyone to be on alert. They should bring back the death penalty and lay his ass six feet under. He does not need to breathe after killing that young boy and I don't want my tax money taking care of a murderer."

I was mad and don't get me wrong, I know the world felt this way but that's somebody's child, my son.

"Excuse me, excuse me," I yelled.

The nurse walked in, "Yes, is everything okay?"

The look on my face should have alerted her that something was indeed wrong, "No, it's not, he is still my son, and if you have children let me give you a piece of advice, don't put your mouth on other people's children or problems because you don't know what your child will do one day, okay."

My blood pressure spiked and the alarm on the machine made a loud noise.

The nurses ran into my room, "Ms. Cole, please calm down."

I yelled at her, "How do you expect me to calm down when you and your co-worker are in the hallway talking about my son!" I was straining my vocal cords and my words were faded.

She was embarrassed and probably afraid that she would get fired if I told her supervisor which I was.

"I'm so sorry we weren't talking about your son."

"You're lying!"

The Dr. came into my room, "is everything okay, what's going on?"

The nurse looked at me scared to death; I took a deep breath to calm my nerves. "I just want to go home."

"Okay, well we have your blood work back and your test was good, it looks like you have high blood pressure. We are going to send you home with some medicine and a prescription and you can go home. Do you have anyone that can pick you up?"

"Yes, I do."

The doctor left out of the room and both nurses looked relieved I didn't get them fired.

One nurse spoke up, "We want to apologize for our unprofessionalism and thank you for not reporting us."

I just shook my head, I wanted to go home, so I called Gary and asked him to come and pick me up.

"I can't Shana, they said we can't leave the house."

"How am I supposed to get home, the hospital is releasing me?"

"They are going to send a police car to get you."

He was kidding me, he had to be kidding me, nope he was not kidding me.

Hours *later*

They released me the next morning after twelve o'clock in the afternoon. I was told to get plenty of rest, I wanted to say, "Doc, there's a manhunt for my son, how am I supposed to rest."

When I stepped outside of the hospital it was beautiful, the sun was out and the warm air felt good against my skin because I was freezing in the hospital.

I thought about Wendell Jr. and how he loved to play outside in this weather. I would walk him to the park, that's before I had a car. It was just me and him and we were happy with each other.

Wendell never wanted to leave me, especially when I dropped him off at daycare. He would cry, and cry but I had to go to work and I didn't have anyone else to watch him.

The police pulled up in an unmarked car just as I was daydreaming. The officer got out and opened my door for me, I thought that was nice of him. I listened to the police radio, and with the crime that goes on in the city, we need the police but we need good, honest nonracist officers.

"Ma'am we're going to do everything we can to bring your son in alive, but it's really up to him."

I looked over at his bald head, I could have slapped him upside the head. Is this all he had to talk about? I didn't say anything, I just kept staring out of the window."

The police car pulled up in front of my house and I saw cops everywhere, they were positioned and ready to shoot. I walked up to my door and I saw a few neighbors looking at me, none of them spoke to me.

As soon as the door opened I smelled Gary's cooking, he cooked the best-fried chicken, better than Popeyes or KFC. "Somethings smells good."

"Mommy," Amanda ran to me, she hugged me so tight.

"Hey, there," I hugged her back, I was working on showing affection.

Gary Jr. walked out of the game room with his headphones around his neck, "hey ma,"

He barely spoke to me, and I felt some kind of way, my feelings were hurt. "What's wrong?"

"I'm missing basketball practice; the coach is not going to let me play if I miss practice. I got to get out of here!"

Gary stepped in, "Wait a minute your mother just got home from the hospital, let her relax. I will talk to the coach; I mean everybody in Delaware knows what's going on."

I walked upstairs to my bedroom and laid down. I was mentally drained but I couldn't stop my brain from thinking about everything.

The next five minutes changed everything. My cell phone rang, I didn't notice the phone number, "hello,"

"Hello, Ma"

My heart dropped and I was happy to hear his voice.

The officer told me to put the phone on speaker, and I did.

"Ma, I can't stay locked up, I can't do prison." He was crying.

"Baby, turn yourself in and we will work something out."

"NO, I'M NOT GOING BACK THERE, THEY CAN KILL ME I DON'T CARE!"

I spoke softly, "I don't want you to die, I love you and I want you to live."

Meanwhile, the police were tracing the call to see where he was.

I could feel my blood pressure rising, and I needed to calm down. "Where are you, I will come to you?"

"I'm in Baltimore but I know you can't come because the police are everywhere looking for me."

"What is the plan, you must have a plan?"

"Yes I do, I'm going to kill anyone that tries to take me in, cops, anybody."

"Wendell you don't mean that."

"Yes, I mean that ma," he hung up the phone.

Just like that, he was gone. I looked at Gary and the police officer and took a deep breath.

The police got to work, and they alerted the Baltimore City, county, and surrounding area to be on the lookout for a tall black male, approximately one hundred and sixty pounds, with black hair and in a stolen red Chrysler 200.

I sat with my head in my hand, shaking my head, I just wanted to know why he did this, and how did he become a killer?"

Three days later

I'm tired of looking at the police outside my door and Gary inside my house. I made him sleep in the guest room; he didn't like it but I didn't care. On the bright side, I was getting phone calls from business owners wanting my accounting services. People were leaving messages.

I couldn't believe the police hadn't arrested him yet.

Later:

It's been seven days since Wendell escaped from a prison van that was taking him to the hospital. I woke up at 8am that morning thinking this had to end. I swung my feet out of bed and opened the blinds to let the sun in and my nosey neighbors stared at my house all the time looking right at me. I didn't want to turn on the tv, because the news media flashed his picture every two seconds, I want this nightmare to be over.

I needed my life back and so did my other children. I sat down at my desk and turned on my computer. I needed to pay some bills and check my website. I logged onto my bank account, and I thought I was seeing things, two thousand dollars was missing from my checking account. I went to the account history and there it was, I knew it, I knew I couldn't trust his ass. I got up and went to the guest room, I grabbed an umbrella from the hall closet first. There it was sleeping on my sheets and enjoying the luxury of my house, comfortably.

I swung the umbrella down on his body with force, "You stole my money!"

He jumped up, "What, Shana, what are you doing?'

"Give me back my money!"

"What money, what are you talking about!"

"You found my bank card and took two thousand dollars out of my account." I was getting ready to hit him again.

"I did not, I've been here with the kids."

Amanda and Gary Jr. run into the guest room, "what's wrong, you woke me up" says Gary Jr.

"Your father stole my money, that was money for my bills."

"Shana wait, I had to pay my car note and car insurance I'm going to give it back."

"Dad, why would you steal from us."

"Your mother has thousands of dollars in the bank she can afford to help me."

I hit him so hard I thought he was unconscious, but he wasn't, he ran and I ran after him.

"Shana, stop you know I can't leave the house."

"No you are getting the fuck out of my house or I am going to have the police arrest you for stealing my money."

I knew that would make him leave, he didn't want any parts of the police with his criminal record.

"Let me get dressed and I will leave."

"Nope, leave just like that."

"I need my shoes; they are my Jordan."

"Good, I can sell them and get some money."

"Shana, don't sell my motherfucking sneakers!"

I can't believe he is worried about a pair of Jordans and not my two thousand dollars.

He left barefoot; I meant what I said.

I slammed the door, "I hate him!"

"Mommy, you hate my dad?'

"Yes, he stole my money, the money I needed to feed and clothe you two!" I knew I shouldn't have said it but I meant it.

The police knocked on the door five minutes later and I was still mad, "what the fuck do you want!"

"They caught your son."

I was scared, "Is he alive?"

The officer shook his head, "Yes, he is alive."

I started hyperventilating, "where did you find him?"

"We caught him in Virginia."

"My son is a man, not an animal, you catch animals, okay."

He kept saying 'we caught," No you did not catch my son. He is not a slave!"

Gary Jr was watching the news and Wendell's arrest was all over the news and so was Sabian's family.

Sabian's mother was speaking to the news media. "I'm glad that monster was caught, he is a monster, just a hateful monster and I wish the police would have killed him! No one should be alive that does the things he does!"

I had no words to say, I would have felt the same way. He was a monster just like my dad and his father.

CHAPTER FIVE

My mother finally came to pick us up after one of the neighbors saw her and told her what was going on in our crack home. You know we lived in that house with no electricity and running water at times for seven years and the neighbors never asked questions or called social services to do a check on us.

You would think we would have been happy to get away from our dad, but the situation was not that much better, you see my mother was an alcoholic, no, she was a drunk, that's just what she was, a drunk. She hung out in bars all night after work, so my sister and I were on our own once again. We had food and clothes but we didn't have love and that is what I needed.

Not having love and not knowing what it really was led me to the arms of Wendell's father, I was fourteen when we met and he was eighteen, he didn't know how old I was, and I looked mature for my age. He was a big-time drug dealer on the streets, he had money and he could have had any woman he wanted but he wanted me. I guess my innocence attracted him to me because I was a virgin. We started dating and he gave me whatever I wanted, and then it came time for me to give him me and I gave it freely because the attention felt good to me. I wasn't getting attention at home and the only attention I got at school was from fights. I had turned into a mean girl but with Wendell, it was different, he made me feel relaxed. He bought me whatever I wanted and I was happy about that.

I missed my period and I started feeling funny, I was eating everything in sight, and my mother fused about that. "Girl you are eaten up everything".

I thought to myself, "Well you haven't fed me in seven years so shut up."

I hadn't been to a doctor in years so I just thought I was sick until I told Wendell I didn't get my period and he said, "You might be pregnant.".

I was in denial at first but then my belly was getting bigger and I felt something moving around. I tried to hide it by wearing big clothes but that didn't help eventually and everyone in school was talking about me.

Yep, I was definitely pregnant and my mother was not happy about it. She didn't want me and my sister living with her and her boyfriend and now I was bringing home a baby at fifteen years old.

Needless to say, she was embarrassed by me but no more than I was about her drunken spells in the street. I used to get teased by the children in the neighborhood. She was a mess when she was drunk and she would become violent to me but not my sister.

My mother praised my sister, everything she did was perfect, she looked perfect, walked, and talked perfectly and especially after I had the baby. I was an embarrassment to her.

It made me feel self-conscious even now 2023 I feel like I'm the ugly duckling and she is the swan because of my mother.

So back to Wendell, we were parents and his mother was all in to have a grandson. Wendell's mother wanted Wendell all of the time at her house, so that gave me a lot of free time to do what I wanted to do, which was run behind her son.

I kept my grades up, that was the only way I could get some recognition from my mother because my sister wasn't and still isn't as smart as I am. Don't get me wrong all of us are gifted and talented, but I am the brains of the bunch.

Wendell and I moved in together, and he paid all of the bills while I went to school. I came home from school and went to Wendell's mother's house to pick up Wendell, and she told me Wendell got locked up and it didn't look good because he had a lot of drugs on him. I was crushed because I didn't want to or should I say I couldn't go back to my mom's house because I burnt the bridge before I left.

She had come home drunk and was acting mean and nasty to me and I had had it, so we started fighting, and she told me to get out and I knew I was never coming back to her house ever again.

Wendell's mother said I could come and stay with her but I was determined to make it on my own, so I dropped out of school and got a job working at a bank. I was making good money and providing for me and my son. I even learned how to drive, got my license, and bought a car. Life was good, real good. However, my son was growing up without a dad because Wendell was sentenced to five years. I took Wendell to see him a few times but I wasn't the prison girlfriend type so I stopped going.

Wendell and I were living great, I worked and made money and took care of my son but I realized I wanted more when a position came up at the bank and I was told I could get it but I needed a GED. I signed up and studied my butt off and I passed it on the first try. I felt like my life was turning around for the good but I was haunted by the abuse from my father and I couldn't get past my mother leaving us. I buried the pain and worked to provide for me and my son.

Wendell was released after serving two and a half years, he came home and things with me were different because I didn't want a drug dealer anymore. I wanted a man that worked and could provide for us and he wasn't trying to hear that. He was a hustler and that was that.

I wasn't alone but I felt lonely and I would get depressed but I didn't know what it was I was feeling.

I had one best friend from high school. Her name was Shameeka but we called her Meeka for short. She and I hung out and we did everything together. Whatever I had I shared with her and vice versa. We were everything my sister and I weren't and would never become. We could and still can confide in one another and there is never judgment between us. She was there doing the highs and lows and basically kept me stable.

I had one male friend, Reginald, he, and I met at work, he was thirteen years older than I was but we had a lot in common he became an uncle to Wendell and a big brother to me.

Meeka and Reggie were my new family, they loved me and Wendell Jr. and we loved them.

Wendell took a turn for the worse; he wasn't making money on the street and he started getting high. Rule number one rule is, don't get high off your own supply. He was smoking crack and he wasn't much of a father to our son and he wasn't giving me money for anything for our son.

Everything was falling on me but I didn't let that stop me. I just kept working and providing. I buried myself in my work just like I did when I was in school, I blocked out my emotions for love and family.

Wendell Jr. was in the second grade and the school had a parent-teacher night, and I asked Wendell to come, and he assured me he would come but I was skeptical because he looked like a crackhead mess. The night of the PTA Wendell didn't show up and Wendell was looking for him, he asked me "Mommy, where is my dad." I had to make up a lie which was one of many after that.

Any feelings I had left for Wendell were gone, I would see him on the street and turn my head because he disgusted me and a part of me felt sorry for him.

My life consisted of work and a little play, Meeka would get me out of the house from time to time and I would mess around with guys here and there but nothing meaningful.

When Gary came into my life I was vulnerable; he was a guy from the neighborhood and after talking to him a few times I thought he was a pretty decent guy. We started out talking on the phone, we would talk every night and he said all the things I wanted to hear, he talked about how he wanted to settle down and get married and he wanted a family. He already had a daughter and he was in her life, something Wendell had no clue on.

After talking to Gary for a few months I felt comfortable with him and I decided to introduce him to Wendell Jr. and they took to each other right away. I was hopeful that this would work but of course, all good things come with some shit and his daughter's mother was the shit that came with him.

I'm a nice person until you continually fuck with me, that's when Sha Sha comes out and she is not nice. Gary's baby momma pushed all of my buttons until I had to snap on her ass. Yes, I had to lay my hands on her to get her to back off. She was used to running other females away but it wasn't so easy.

I hadn't heard from Gary for a few days and Meeka told me he got locked up, soon after she told me he called and explained that he had some trouble with this guy and he was fighting. I believed him and when he called from prison I took his calls. I was by myself once again. I couldn't hang in there with him because I had to get money. That's all I thought about day and night was making money so I could have all the things I ever wanted as a child, all the things I dreamed of, I was working towards getting. I didn't have to wish and hope or be jealous of other people anymore because I was getting what I wanted.

I heard my father had moved to Atlanta and right after my sister graduated from high school she moved to Atlanta.

I thought about what was in Delaware and it wasn't much so I decided I was going to move too, but Gary asked me to wait until he came home from prison because he wanted to marry me.

I never dreamed of getting married; he had three years and I thought to myself that's not a long time, so I waited.

When he came home he proposed to me.

"Did you love him?"

"Dr. Parker, honestly, I didn't know what love looked like, smelled like, or anything. I was just happy I was asked, and besides Wendell Jr. was getting a father".

By this time, my father had gotten his life together in Georgia, he had gone to rehabilitation for crack, came out got married, and was working with Liberty Taxes.

My father reached out to me and I told him I was getting married and he said he would pay for everything even though I wanted to keep it simple.

That's the dad I remembered, giving and supportive.

The wedding was beautiful and both of our families were there. I had on a beautiful dress; I mean my father spared no expense on my wedding. It was my fairytale wedding. Everything before that day didn't exist, or so I thought.

Once we got married I was ready to move to Atlanta, I wanted to get Gary away from Delaware because he was fucking up, every day it was everything but a steady job.

I couldn't do the in and out of prison so I told him I was moving to Atlanta and he could stay or go but I was leaving Delaware.

"Okay, Shana I think that is enough for this session, I will schedule you for next week."

"Dr. Parker, do you think I'm making progress because coming to you and reliving my life is not helping me."

"This is your third time here and we have a lot more sessions to go but you will see a breakthrough, I promise.

Leaving her office felt like leaving the dentist after getting a tooth pulled, I was in pain but I was going to trust the process.

After turning on my phone I saw I had a bunch of missed calls, I could only hope they were work-related and after listening to them, thank God they were.

Two weeks later

I hadn't heard from Wendell, no calls or anything so I called the prison to find out why. They told me he was on lock up in a Maximum prison in Baltimore because he hit an officer and stabbed another inmate.

I shook my head, "how did he get a knife in prison?"

I hated going to visit him in prison, I couldn't bare seeing him caged up, like an animal. I know some mothers are thankful they can visit their sons; I mean at least he wasn't dead but what do you call a prison cell? I call it a coffin, it's no better than going to a grave site. I can't touch him or hug him. All I can do is look at his face through a glass window, there's no life in his eyes anymore and I don't know who he is.

The visit.

Business was booming but I wasn't surprised; I was booked and busy. My appointment book was filled for up to two months and the word was getting around even to other states. My website did the trick.

It was the middle of the week and I didn't have any appointments until Friday. I decided to ride to Baltimore and visit Wendell. I hated coming to Baltimore City it looked like a third-world Country and I thought Delaware was bad, oh my goodness. I stopped at a light on North and Howard Street and a young man walked up to me with a bottle of Windex I guess and a squeegee and asked if I wanted my window cleaned. I politely said no and he cussed me out, he called me a bitch and spit on my window. I wanted to jump out and kick his minor ass but I heard too much about Baltimore City to do that. I couldn't wait until the light turned green.

I turned down Greenmount Avenue and I saw a prison over here, over there, and everywhere, damn, I didn't see a school at all. I shook my head and found a place to park.

I went into the prison, gave my name, and was escorted to the visiting room. I sat down and waited for them to bring Wendell out. I was on pins and needles waiting.

The officer came back and I looked and Wendell wasn't with him.

"Where is my son?"

"I'm sorry ma'am but he refused the visit."

"Why," I couldn't believe he didn't want to see me.

"He's on a hunger strike and he said he didn't want any visits."

"A hunger strike, what the hell for," I thought to myself.

I looked at the officer dumbfounded and concerned "Why is he doing this!"

"Ma'am inmates do this all the time when they can't do what they want."

"What does he want?"

The officer looked at me as if I was stupid as hell, "He wants what every inmate wants, to leave ma'am."

Okay, I got up and left the visiting room, I'm not going to lie I wasn't disappointed, it's hard enough seeing him.

On my way home it started raining, I hate driving in the rain. All the way home I thought about him starving himself, and I started praying for him and using the meditation tools Dr. Parker taught me.

I drove up to the toll booth and realized I didn't have any money to pay with. I told the toll worker and she let me know in a nasty tone, "You're going to get a big bill in the mail."

"Oh shut the hell up," I wanted to say.

When I crossed into Delaware I felt a dip in my stomach like something was wrong, my cell phone rang, I looked down at the phone and it was Amanda's school calling.

"Is this Ms. Cole?"

I'm panicking, "Yes, yes, is everything okay?"

"Amanda got into a fight with another student and we need you to come up to the school."

I told them I was on my way, damn can I catch a break, I hit the steering wheel.

This wasn't like Amanda to get into a fight and the sad part about it is, I couldn't call that thief of a father of hers. I wish he would have stayed in Georgia instead of following behind me.

When I arrived at the school I wasn't expecting anything serious, however, I was in for a shock.. I walked into a mess.

"Mrs. Cole have a seat please."

I sat down and looked around, "where is my daughter?"

"We had to call the police."

I jumped up, "the police, she's only nine years old."

"Calm down Mrs. Cole and let me explain."

"I want my daughter right now, take me to her before I turn this place upside down and inside out!"

"Alright, alright."

"You called the police on my little girl, why because she's black!" I saw her turn pink in the face and I didn't care.

"Mrs. Cole your daughter stabbed a little girl with a pencil repeatedly."

I sat down in shock, "is the little girl okay, what happened? Amanda is not violent. Just as I was about to go up in my thoughts the police brought Amanda into the room. I grabbed her and hugged her and then I looked her over to make sure they didn't hurt her.

She hugged me so tight, she was afraid of the police, "Mommy she started it."

"What happened Amanda?"

The principal quickly interrupted her and started explaining what happened.

"Excuse me, I'm not talking to you, I want to hear what my daughter has to say."

I sat back down in the chair, "look at me, tell me your side of the story."

Her eyes were red from crying, "I was minding my business and then Katelin started yelling at me and saying mean things about Wendell."

"Did you tell the teacher?"

"My teacher heard her; the class heard her and they were laughing and I asked them to stop but they kept laughing and she kept calling him a killer and a jailbird."

I took a deep breath because I was mad and not at Amanda, Baby I will take care of it, okay."

The principal looks at me, "The family wants to press charges against her."

"She's nine and besides they were mentally abusing her and the teacher did nothing. I am going to sue this school and have the news media up here!"

"Your little girl stabbed her, Mrs. Cole, you're being unfair."

I looked at Amanda, "was she black or white?"

The principal's face turned from pink to red.

"She was white."

"That's exactly what I thought, you let a white child mentally torment my daughter in front of a classroom full of students and a teacher and you expect her not to react!"

"Ms. Cole, think about it, she stabbed her."

"If I humiliate you, taunt you, and embarrass you in front of your peers what would you do?"

"Well, I doubt very seriously if I would stab you."

I wanted to say, "bitch please."

"She may need therapy; a lot has happened within your family."

She was right, Amanda did need therapy, "I will get her in therapy."

"Would you like to know how Katelin is doing?"

Yeah, I did, "yes."

"She is fine, the pencil didn't break her skin."

I was laughing to myself, "Okay, that's good."

Amanda and I walked to the car and a police officer followed us.

"Are they going to lock me up?"

"Of course not, besides over my damn body."

"What is therapy?"

On our way home I explained to her what therapy was and I told her that I was in therapy with the hopes that would make her feel better. I wanted to tell her next time don't stab anyone, instead smack the shit out of them, but I didn't.

I stopped off to get us something to eat and as soon as I ordered the food I thought about Wendell, he loved cheesesteak subs. I could get him to do anything around the house if I promised him a cheese steak sub. Now my baby is not eating at all. I shook my head and ordered our food.

I called Gary Jr's cell phone to see what he wanted to eat but I didn't get an answer, come to think of it I hadn't talked to him all day. That was odd, Gary Jr. always texts me throughout the day. I went ahead and ordered food for all of us.

We pulled up to the house and I was happy to be home. I had one hell of a day; I can try and enjoy this sub that I didn't need but was going to anyway.

I walked into the kitchen from the garage and flipped the lights on, Amanda and I screamed, "Who are you and what the hell are you doing in my kitchen?"

"Hi my name is Holly, she waved, "Gary told me I could get some water from the refrigerator, I was thirsty."

I covered Amanda's eyes because Holly was naked, "Gary, Gary, get your butt down here right now!"

I sent Amanda up to her room while I handled whatever this was.

Gary Jr. comes down the stairs wearing his boxers, no t-shirt, and a smile, "Yeah ma what's up."

"Why is this girl standing in my clean kitchen with no clothes on, and why is she even at my house without me being here?"

I looked at Holly's pale skin, "Go get your clothes so you can leave."

"Okay," she runs upstairs, leaving me with a vision of a flat ass.

Gary Jr tries to leave with her, "Oh no, you stay your ass right here. Have you lost your mind bringing a girl into my house and fucking her!"

"You're just saying that because she's white."

"I wouldn't give a damn if she was green, you don't fuck in my house."

"Dad lets me bring girls to his apartment."

Now he just told me something because I didn't know that, of course, I didn't know because Gary would never tell me that. "I don't care what you do at your father's apartment but in my house, that is a hell no."

"Mommy, I'm hungry," Amanda yells from upstairs.

I ignored her because I had to deal with this fool, "Didn't you know I was coming home?"

"Yes, but I'm seventeen, you know I'm having sex."

My armpits immediately started to sweat, I needed to take several deep breaths now because I didn't want to say the wrong thing however, I did just walk in with a white girl butt ass naked in my refrigerator.

Amanda stumps her foot on the floor, "Mommy, I'm hungry now."

The two of them had hit the last nerve, "Get your ass in your room until I come and get you!"

I could hear her crying and screaming like the spoiled brat her father had created but I didn't care.

"Go upstairs and get dressed and we will discuss this after she leaves."

Gary Jr. startles me with this, "I want to go and live with Dad, he said he was going to buy me a car and I would rather live with him anyway."

What did my ungrateful son just say to me? He wants to live with his dad, that man ain't got a pot to piss in or a window to throw it out of but you know what I'm going to let him go.

I was calm, "Go right ahead, go live with your dad," I said sarcastically, "I think that's a good idea, and he's going to buy you a car that's even better."

I surprised his ass for sure because he thought I gave a damn but there was no reason for me to stop him.

"Are you serious Mom?"

I sat down in the kitchen at the island and started unwrapping my sub, "Yep I'm serious, go right ahead, and after you pack I'll drive you over there."

He was happy, and all smiles, I chuckled, poor thing he was getting ready to get a reality check, "Oh, and one more thing."

"What's that?"

"Stop messing around with them, stay with your own kind, and wear a condom, I want to see you succeed with a black woman."

Snow White just so happened to hear me, she had a dumb look on her face, but I did not care, I said what I said.

Gary Jr. walked Holly to her car.

I peeped out to watch them; he kissed her on the lips. I shook my head, "when will they learn."

He came back in and asked if he could use my good suitcase. I told him absolutely not and handed him some trash bags.

He looked at me as if to say are you serious?

And my look back to him was damn right, "You're not going on a vacation, you're moving out, son."

I called Amanda downstairs to get her sub and she and I sat at the island and ate while Gary Jr, aka, dumb ass went upstairs to stuff the trash bags.

He came downstairs with five bags, "I'm hungry did you bring me a sub?"

I handed him his sub and chuckled to myself, I said to myself, "Enjoy because that may be your last good meal."

He loaded my truck and I drove him thirty minutes to his father's apartment. I didn't ask him if his father knew he was coming, I guess he cleared it with him.

We pulled up to Gary's apartment and Gary Jr called him from his cell phone.

"Dad, I'm out front, I got all my stuff."

I acted like I was listening.

We saw Gary looking out of his blinds

"There's Daddy," Amanda pointed up to the window.

"Go ahead get your stuff out the back, your father will help you with the bags.

Apparently, Gary Sr. didn't have a clue his son was on the way. Those two are just alike, they talk a lot of shit and then need someone to clean it up.

Gary Jr looked over at me, "he's coming to the truck."

"Get your stuff so I can pull off." I didn't want to see him.

"Wait, Mommy, I want to see my daddy."

 Apparently, Amanda did.

He walked out to the truck with shorts, a t-shirt, and slippers, "Hey, what happened."

I didn't say one word.

Gary Jr. took a deep breath, "Mom said I could live with you.

"I did not say that!" lying ass boy just like his father, damn. "You told me you were moving out because your father was buying you a car and you can fuck bitches in his apartment!"

Gary Sr. looked at his son as if to say, boy, you fucked up and pissed your mother off, don't you know that's my job."

I told him to get out of my car so I could pull off.

He unloaded my car and Amanda wanted some attention from her father but he was too busy trying to figure fatherhood out in his head.

"Daddy, I want a hug and a kiss."

Gary Sr. walked up to the truck and hugged her, "I love you sunshine."

"I love you too, and I'm going to come move with you too."

I turned around and looked at her, "what!"

She was all smiles, but she wasn't going anywhere.

Gary looked dumbfounded as hell; I saw the lump in his throat.

"You stay with mommy, the boys over here, and the girls at mommy's house, okay."

She shook her head in agreement.

"Shanna can I speak to you for a minute," he started to walk around to the driver's side and I put my car in D and drove off. I didn't even look in my rearview mirror.

Later that night I put Amanda to bed and I overheard her saying her prayers.

"God please take care of my brothers; let Wendell Jr. be good in prison and I pray that Gary Jr. becomes a professional football player or a stockbroker and let daddy and mommy like each other again."

I went into my room and had a talk with God, "I'm tired God, actually I'm exhausted."

CHAPTER SIX

DON'T GET COMFORTABLE.

Gary Jr thought he was being slick by moving in with his father but he will see just how much of an asshole his father is, the only person Gary ever cared about was himself.

Dr. Parker's left eyebrow went up, "So how was the marriage?

I wanted to move away from Delaware after we got married and I realized it would be a change, for sure. I was picking up my life the only life I had ever known and moving to a new normal so I thought.

I, Gary, and Wendell packed up and drove to Atlanta but I didn't tell Gary I was pregnant. I wanted to wait until we had finished the move. Things started out okay, my good job allowed me to transfer to Atlanta and Gary was driving trucks, he had his CDL license. My sister said we could move with her until we found a place.

One day I was driving in Conyers Ga, it's not too far from Atlanta and I saw a new housing development. I made up my mind right then and there that I was going to get one of those homes. I worked and Gary worked and we saved every penny we could.

My sister was nice enough not to charge us anything but I didn't want to overstay my welcome.

I was getting bigger so I told Gary I was pregnant, he was excited about it, actually, we both were excited about it.

Shortly after I found out I was pregnant we went looking at houses. We applied for a loan for the house and we got it. Every day I would drive to the site and watch them build my dream home. I dreamt of owning a home and decorating it for the holidays and it was coming true. Gary and I picked out the designs and the layout for the rooms. I had to pinch myself because everything was going so good.

My father and I were bonding over taxes, he knew I was excellent with numbers and I caught on right away. I was working at the bank, working in the tax office, and pregnant all at the same time. I didn't have time for anything or anyone. I may have seen Wendell a few times during the week but Gary stepped up and he was right there to pick up the slack by taking him to games and doing things with him.

That's when I learned things can't stay good forever, Meeka called me and told me Gary had a son from this girl in Delaware. I told her that couldn't be true because he's been with me but Meeka swore it was true and because she is my best friend she wouldn't lie to me.

I asked Gary about it and he told me he didn't know anything about it and I believed him.

We were moving into our new home with our new baby. I named him after Gary, Gary Jr. but we weren't the only ones having a baby; My father's wife Mildred was having a baby also. I swear when my father told me she was pregnant I was hurt, he was my dad, and now he was going to be someone else's father. I know I shared him with my sister and brother but I didn't want to share him with anyone else.

Mildred was a snooty bitch and she was a recovering addict too. Like how do you be snooty and you used to smoke crack, that shit doesn't even go together, but she and my father had it all. The tax business was profitable for my dad, he had seven stores and he was making a lot of money. He and Mildred lived in a house bigger than mine and they drove luxury cars. Every time I saw Mildred looked expensive and she looked down at me and my sister. She didn't know the monster we knew and now they were building a family.

Our home was perfect and we were perfect so I thought. We weren't in our home a month before papers came from Delaware for child support for Gary Sr's illegitimate son. The whore dared to name him Gary Cole Jr.

Devastated, that's the only word I had to describe the pain in my heart and then another court order for child support came for his daughter in Delaware. The bridge was tumbling down on him and because I was married to him, me too.

I was furious with him, but I couldn't cry and I didn't. I felt betrayed because I married this man and this is what he did to our marriage. He repeatedly said it was not his child, but "nigga you fucked her! The question of you being the father shouldn't be a factor."

I was living in my dream home and in a sinkhole at the same time, but I threw all of my focus into the jobs. I became a beast with taxes, I was taking over and my father didn't care because he was reaping the benefits and growing his family.

When it was time for Gary Sr. to go to child support court I went with him. I wanted to see this woman that he fucked after he married me. I guess a part of me wanted to see if I measured up to her if anything.

We drove eighteen hours to Delaware the day before court, I brought Wendell Jr. along because he wanted to see his father. I didn't know what shape Wendell Sr. was in but I agreed to let him see his father's family.

I should have gone with my first instinct because Wendell Sr. was worse than before. I had never seen him so far gone on drugs.

When Wendell Sr. saw our son he didn't know who he was, he asked, "Who are you?"

My son was crushed.

Meeka went to court with me for backup just in case anything popped off.

Gary and I were on one side and she was on the other side of the courtroom. I looked her up and down and then I looked at him, "Really, you could have leveled up."

Gary asked for a blood test and she went completely off in the courtroom, she had to be restrained.

I looked at her, "Like bitch you do not want this."

She got herself together and agreed to the blood test.

On the way out of the courtroom, she walked up close to me, "I fucked your husband and we have a child."

I could have killed the bitch with my bare hands, she wanted Sha Sha to come raging out, but I had too much to lose so I hit her with, yep you fucked my husband and he will remain my husband and your son will never be a part of this family. You got a son but he will not have a daddy." I meant that shit too and I told Gary if this is your son, he will not come anywhere near me or this family. Don't speak his name around me ever.

He promised me it wasn't his baby, and thirty days later the test results came back 99.99%. That's when things changed between us, I went numb and I told him he and I would never be the same.

There were three Gary's and two Gary Jrs. Talk about a nightmare with your eyes open.

My sister decided to move to Florida after her breakup with her first husband. I felt like I wasn't needed in her life anymore and we were starting to bond.

I was going to miss her and my niece, my namesake but at least I had somewhere to visit.

Our home was beautiful but our marriage was ugly. I worked around the clock to pay the house bills because his check was going to child support for two children outside of our home so where did that leave our kids.

Gary wanted to get his daughter Aisha for the summer. I thought it would be a good thing to have all the kids together but it turned out to be another disaster.

Gary treated his daughter better than the other children and that caused a division between him and Wendell Jr.

When Aisha came to Georgia, she had her own room and I bought her clothes, I was excited but that soon changed when she gave me her ass to kiss. I was doing everything to accept his daughter and make her feel comfortable but nothing worked. She was rattling my cage and Gary defended her with everything.

I gave up trying to appease her and focused on work.

The next few years my dad and Mildred were pumping babies out one by one, my dad was so focused on his new family. Mildred gave him two girls and a son, just as my mother had and it was in the same order. I couldn't believe it.

"What feelings did you have about that?"

"Dr. Parker, honestly I was jealous."

How could he give them the life he should have given us, why would God do that to me and my siblings? We got a monster, my mother got a shitty husband and now God gives him a new life, wife, and children, that wasn't fair.

I had two miscarriages back-to-back, and I was depressed but I didn't know I was depressed if that made any sense. I threw myself into work even more. When tax season was over I started working for businesses and when they didn't have work for me, I started taking online business classes. I was moving like a machine and everyone around me was happy.

Gary got hurt on the job and they prescribed him Oxycodone, and at the time we just thought it was pain pills but just like everyone else we found out it was more.

I saw the change in him but I was too wrapped up in my own world to care.

After a while, it all came crashing down, I found the pill bottles and the prescription pad. I stared at it for a few minutes, trying to decide what to do. I called my sister but she never answered, and then I called my best friend Meeka and told her and she told me to put him out of the house.

"Did you do that?"

Dr. Parker I packed up all of his shit and had it waiting for him at the door, I even got him a hotel room so he could have a place to go.

"Wait say that again, you put him out and get him a hotel room?"

"That sounds crazy doesn't it?"

"No, but it's not normal, I'll say that. We are going to stop right here and pick up next week."

It was still light outside and it was a beautiful day, the sun was beaming. I had a few hours before I had to pick up Amanda and my work calendar was clear, so I put on my dark blue Balenciaga sunglasses and drove to the riverside in Wilmington to get something to eat and walk on the docks and clear my head.

Come to think about it, I haven't enjoyed a walk, a run, or anything since Wendell, I get choked up just thinking about him killing that young boy.

I walked into Timothy's Grill and before I could order I felt someone standing close up on me so I turned around quickly.

"Hello, I'm sorry I was trying to remember your name."

It was the officer who let me go with no insurance, "Hello, it's Shana, Shana Cole."

He extended his hand, "Hell Ms. Cole my name is Michael."

I smiled, and extended my hand, "Hi Michael, I have insurance now do you want to see?"

Michael laughed, "I trust you, but just in case let me see."

I looked at him, and then I reached into my purse to show him my proof of insurance.

"No, no I was joking, besides I'm off duty."

There was an awkward silence until the waiter asked me for my order.

I ordered a grilled chicken sandwich on a bun with lettuce, tomatoes, mayo, onions, and chips, and a large water with lemon.

Michael leans in from behind me, and hands the waiter his debit card, "Here, I'll pay for her bill."

I was offended, "You don't have to do that."

He smiled at me, "I know, I want to do it."

I couldn't help but think he was feeling sorry for me.

"Did you follow me here?"

"No, I was sitting over there having a late lunch and I saw you pull up and I remembered your Georgia tags GODBLES."

"Ohhhhhh, okay," that was a relief, I thought to myself.

"Would you like to join me?"

I froze, Jesus Christ, what is going on here, what do I do?

I looked dumb I know it, "Sure, I can join you at your table."

He told the waiter to bring my food to his table.

I was nervous because I haven't had attention like this from a man in years, maybe not years but it's been a while. I walked in front of him to his table and he pulled my chair out, Lord, what was going on.

Once I sat down I didn't know what to say, I sat there looking stupid and clutching my purse.

"After you pulled off that night I couldn't stop thinking about you, or should I say how you were crying."

"I had a rough day, and a ton of things going on."

"I felt that that's why you were on my mind. I wanted to reach out to you but I didn't want to abuse my police powers."

He bit his sandwich and for a second I stared at him as his chewed gazing at his big lips, they were just the right size to kiss.

He caught me gazing, "is something wrong,"

"No, no, I'm just hungry," I looked for the waiter to see if my food was coming.

"Are you alright," he looked concerned.

Let me be honest with him, "I'm nervous, I haven't been, you know, you know."

He laughs, "I know what."

"I haven't sat across from a man and ate in a long time, I'm recently divorced."

He put his sandwich down, and wiped his lips and hands on his napkin, "I haven't sat across from a beautiful queen in a long time."

I wanted to throw up, not this man is not trying to run a game on me!

"What about your mom and sisters?"

"I grew up in foster care, with no real mother, and as far as I know I am an only child."

Ewwww, that's not good, I thought to myself. "I'm sorry to hear that."

"No, don't be, I'm fine, I'm in therapy to work out all of the kinks in my head."

Wait, did he just say he is in therapy.

"I learned after a divorce and other losses that I needed therapy."

"Do you tell all the strangers you meet that you are in therapy?"

Michael smiled, "No, only the strangers that I would like to become friends with."

Geez he had pretty teeth, I nodded my head and smiled back. Finally, my food was brought to the table. "I don't want to hold you up, you're almost finished eating."

"I don't have anywhere I need to be."

"Do you have any children," I asked him.

"I do, my ex-wife and I have four sons."

My eyes stretched opened wide, "four sons, that sounds like a hand full."

"I would rather have sons than raise daughters. I would have to shoot one of these fools out here, what about you how many children do you have?"

I had just bitten into my sandwich and I didn't want to talk with food in my mouth, so I put up my finger. I have three two boys and one girl and I am divorced as well."

"Would you ever get married again?"

Wow, he came straight at me, I had to catch my breath.

"Go ahead and enjoy your food, I'll wait."

The way he looked at me when he said that I ain't going lie, made my panties wet but thank goodness he stopped talking because I was hungry. I took my time and enjoyed my grilled chicken sandwich and it was delicious too.

It was kinda hard to eat while he was looking at me and talking to me.

"I know you must think I do this often?"

"What walk up to women you have pulled over and buy them lunch and then tell them all of your business, yeah." I had to laugh.

And so did he, he was laughing so hard that the people around us started looking.

"You are something else, I love a woman with a sense of humor and honest."

I chuckled, "Is that right."

"You are a beautiful woman, and I felt your pain the night I pulled you over."

"Yeah," I lowered my head.

"I would like to get to know you if that's okay with you."

"What are you asking me," I'm not reading between the lines, he's going to have to say it.

"Can I take you out on a date?"

I love the confidence, "let me think about it but I will give you my phone number."

He nodded his head, "Okay, I respect that."

I looked at my watch, "I have to pick my daughter up from daycare."

I took his phone number and when I pushed my seat back he jumped up to pull my seat out. This dude is really trying to impress me but why is he divorced if he's a nice guy. "Thank you."

I pulled my sunshades from my Walmart purse and put them on and gave the sexiest walk I possibly could.

"Wait," he yelled.

I turned around.

"You didn't give me your number."

"I know, you'll get it when or if I call you." I turned back around and walked to my car and I'm not going to lie, I felt so powerful. I felt in control and I needed that because I can't ever be weak again.

I got in my car and when I looked up and he was staring at me smiling, wow I didn't see this in my day at all.

It was getting late so called the daycare to let them know I was on my way to pick up Amanda only to have them tell me that she wasn't there. "What, where is she!"

Apparently, she was picked up by her father and he failed to communicate with me that he was going to pick her up. Ohhhhhh, he makes me so damn mad.

I called him, I didn't wait for him to say hello, "Why did you pick her up without asking me?"

"Excuse me, don't yell at me, I'm a grown-ass man and that is my daughter too. I don't have to ask you. I'm paying child support so I can see her whenever I want to!"

"We don't have joint custody Gary for a reason, so bring her home right now!"

"Fuck you Shana, I'll bring her home when I get ready." He hangs up the phone.

I was mad, this is just like him to do some dumb shit but I'm tired of his shit, I'm exercising all of my power. I called 911.

"I need a police officer; my daughter was picked up by her father from daycare without my permission and I have sole custody of her and now he's telling me he is not bringing her home."

"Do you have proof on you that you have sole custody?"

"Yes, I do," I opened my glove box and pulled it out, thank goodness I keep it with me.

"What is the address, ma'am?"

"3400 Miller Rd at 202"

"We'll send someone to meet you there."

Why did Gary do this? He is always breaking the rules and then telling me he's changed. I hate for baby girl to see her father in handcuffs but that's what it's going to be if he doesn't give me my daughter.

I pulled up before the police, how the hell did that happen anyway, I banged on his door.

"Stop banging on my door Shana," he opened the door.

I'm not going in there; I just came to get my daughter.

"Where is she?"

"She's in the bathroom,"

I peeped into the apartment and he had a bitch in there with her daughter. "Why did you go and pick her up without asking me?"

He tried to flex on me, I guess trying to impress her.

"Me and my girl went to pick her up so we could take them out to the park and get something to eat."

She looked at me, "Like bitch what is your problem?"

That was the wrong motherfucking look to give me.

I went in on Gary, "Don't go breaking the rules trying to impress a bitch you ain't going to be with a week. This is the stuff I'm talking about when you tell me you've changed. I don't know her and you got my baby around her!"

"She's my daughter too Shana." He slammed the door in my face.

Finally, the police roll up, and good because I'm ready to kick this motherfucking door in.

The officer walked up to me, "Ms. we got a call about a disturbance,"

"What, I called because my daughter is in there without my permission."

The officer ignored me, "A call came in and said you were banging on the door and causing problems."

I took a deep breath and calmed myself down, "Officer I called the police over thirty minutes ago, my daughter was picked up from daycare by her father without my permission and I have sole custody."

The officer knocks on the door.

Gary opens the door, "I called, officer."

Amanda saw me and ran to me, "Mommy, come meet my new friend, Casey," she grabs my hand.

"No, get your book bag and come on."

"Wait ma'am, I need to talk to him before you can take her."

"I don't know what kind of games you are playing sir, but I have papers showing I have full custody, what he did today was kidnapping."

I look and see two other cops pulled up, hopefully, they were my cops.

I had to look twice, Michael, what in the heck was he doing here.

"Hello did you call about your daughter taken from daycare?"

"Yes, yes I did."

Michael looked at me, and then he walked over to me, "This is awkward isn't it, we were just having lunch together and now this."

I was too embarrassed to say anything.

"Hey," he touched my arm, "what's going on talk to me."

"I went to pick up my daughter and they told me my ex had picked her up and I have full custody and he can't pick her up unless I okay it, which I did not."

Michael walked over to Gary, "Sir do you have joint custody with your daughter's mother?'

"No, but"

Michael cut him right off, "If you don't then you can't pick her up from anywhere at any time, or you are violating a court order. If she wants to press charges we are going to have to arrest you right now."

Bitch ass Gary looked at me, I was so mad at myself because once again I felt sorry for him. I didn't want Amanda to see him get arrested she would never forgive me for that. "No, I'm not going to press charges.

"Sir are you going to press charges on her for disturbing the peace," asked the first officer that came.

"Yes, I am."

Wait, what the fuck just happened here, "Gary are you crazy?"

"No, I'm not crazy, but you're not going to come to my apartment and act a fool in front of my girl. You need to respect the fact that I have moved on."

I was paralyzed, I could move, speak, or breathe, how could I be so dumb once again. He stole from me countless times and I never called the police on him and he wants me arrested.

"Ma'am put your hands behind your back," says the police.

"Wait, man, she just let you off the hook for kidnapping and now you want her arrested, hell no, don't cuff her. What kind of father are you to do this in front of your kid."

Michael was standing up for me, and it was the first time anyone had ever stood up for me.

Gary gave me a hard look.

"Let her go, babe."

"I won't press charges," says Gary.

Wow, she feels important I bet, but I shook my head because she has no idea what awaits her.

I grabbed Amanda's hand and walked quickly to my car when I heard Michael call my name.

"Ms. Cole, can I speak to you for a minute?"

I turned around with an attitude, "I guess you think I owe you?"

"No not at all."

"I thought you were off today."

"A police officer is never really off the clock. I got a call to come and help out because they are short and so I came and I'm glad I did."

"Yeah well now you know, I was married to an asshole."

"So was I but that is our past."

He opened my car door for me to put Amanda in her car seat and then walked around to open my driver's door. I looked up and saw Gary staring out of the window watching my every move.

I thanked Michael again and drove off.

CHAPTER SEVEN

There are some of the things I missed about Georgia, the great weather and the many choices to eat but above all, I miss the people. The people in Georgia were so nice and cordial including the white people. Delaware people never change, grumpy, tired, and boring but I chose to move back so I guess I'll have to deal with it.

It was May and Delaware's weather was tricky, the mornings were brisk, the afternoons were warm and the nights were cool.

Once I got Amanda off to school I went out on the deck and enjoyed the morning air and sipped my coffee. I took my laptop so I could plan my schedule for the weeks ahead. I never saw my business doing so well so soon but I was thankful it was.

It was hard enjoying success when I had a son wasting away in a prison cell, every time I try to have a good day my mind takes me to Wendell and I'm not going to lie I think about Sabian and his family. "God, my son is a murderer!" I screamed inside my head; I slammed my laptop, I felt sick, my stomach knotted up, and it happened every time I thought about it.

It's been months, and I needed to go back to Baltimore and see how my son was coping inside there, but I didn't want to imagine how he was coping.

Just as I was about to step into the shower my cell phone rang and it was Gary Jr. I looked over at the clock and grabbed my phone to answer it.

I barely said hello before he started talking.

"Ma, I need some money for my graduation dues, they are due this week and if I don't pay them I can't participate in the graduation."

Wait, didn't this boy move out and tell me his father got him, now he needed my help. "Gary J. you need to ask your father, you live with him remember, he's responsible for your well-being. That was the decision you made."

"Ma come on, I need the money, Dad don't have no money."

Correct yourself, It's Dad doesn't have any money,"

"Ma really, I don't have time for a grammar lesson, this is serious."

What he didn't realize is that I wasn't giving him shit. He was just like his dad, treating me like shit and then needing me.

"I'm not giving you money; you live with your father and it's his responsibility to take care of those things, didn't he just buy you a car?"

Silence, he didn't say one word.

"Hello, did you get your car?"

"No, ma please I have to graduate, I'll do whatever you want, please pay it for me."

I needed a minute to talk to myself and use the tools Dr. Parker gave me.

"No, I'm not giving you any money, Gary J."

"Ma, stop playing, I need to participate in the graduation. If I don't I'll be humiliated."

I'd had enough of going back and forth with him, "Gary J I said no, I'm not going to give you the money. Get it from your father, make him responsible."

"If you don't give me the money I am going out here and do something crazy to get the money!"

A lump the size of a bowling ball formed in my throat; did I just hear him right. I froze, the shower water steamed up the bathroom, and I couldn't see my reflection in the mirror. Before I knew it I was sitting on the floor of my bathroom rocking and thinking where did I go wrong.

"Ma, Ma, are you there!"

I had to find my voice, but I couldn't; I hung up the phone.

I sat on the floor crying, rocking, and wondering why my God would give me evil children, and just then, my father's sins flashed before me.

My father was a mean, vile, selfish son of a bitch and the only person he cared about was himself and what do you know I married a man just like him and reproduced.

I went into a deep depression, I didn't want to work or talk to anyone, I just wanted to die.

The days and weeks after were a blur, I couldn't or should I say I didn't want to get out of bed and poor Amanda was taking care of herself; I had nothing not even a care.

Weeks later, Sunday Morning

I woke to the smell of bacon, and I heard voices. I jumped out of bed and walked into the kitchen looking like a homeless woman. I saw Meeka and Reginald cooking while Amanda was sitting eating and laughing.

Meeka looked at me, "Good Morning" she smiled.

"How did you get in my house?"

"Our Goddaughter called us and we came right over," says Reggie.

"Who opened the door for you," I looked at Amanda.

"Girl, did you forget I have a key, and I used it."

I stared at them, I was two seconds away from crying when Meeka walked over to me and hugged me so tight.

She whispered, "We are here, we got you."

I pushed her away and walked back to my room. No one has ever had me; I've always had to have myself. I got back in my bed.

Meeka took Amanda with her to her house and it was best because I couldn't fight the depression I was in.

Before I knew it, it was June, and days before Gary Jr's graduation. Everyone from Dr. Parker to Gary Jr and his father was blowing up my phone along with my mother but I didn't care whether he graduated or not. I was curled up in my bed and only thinking about the one person no one else thought about, I was putting myself first for once.

What I really wanted was a do-over, but God couldn't give me that.

Juneteenth there was a hard knock at my door.

I walked to the door in my robe and slippers, my hair looked a mess, and I smelled from lack of bathing. I looked through the peephole and it was the police, I panicked and grabbed my chest, "Why are they here?"

The officer pounded on the door again, "Ms. Cole, are you in there?"

"Yes, what do you want?"

"Open the door ma'am it's the police."

I shook my head like I gave two fucks about it being the police. "What do you want!"

"We're here to do a wellness check ma'am."

I cracked the door open just enough for them to see my face, "A wellness check on who, who told you to come here?"

"Ma'am we got a call to come by and check on you, you're mother called the police."

I said to myself, "My mother," now she's worried about me. I needed her to send the police when I was five years old, not now.

"Officer I am fine, you can tell her that I am fine, okay." I closed the door.

A knock at the door, again "Shana it's me, Michael."

What on earth was he doing at my house, I sure as hell wasn't about to open the door for him.

"Shana, open up, we have to come in for a wellness check."

"This is some bullshit," as my ex-coworker Brenda would say.

I opened the door and let both the officers in, "You see I'm fine."

Michael stared at me, he didn't look around he just stared at me, I was offended.

"Why are you staring at me like that?"

"I'm sorry, are you okay?"

"Yes, yes I'm okay, now can you two please leave." I'm annoyed and I want them to know I'm annoyed.

Michael turns to the other officers and whispers something to him and then the other officer leaves.

"Shana, what's going on?"

"Michael, no disrespect but you don't know me, and I don't know you. So don't come in my house acting like some white knight that came to save my life," I broke down into tears.

Michael took two steps toward me and I was in his big strong arms once again, what in the hell was going on. I cried and cried until snot came out of my nose, my bonnet came off of my head and my robe fell open. I was completely open and vulnerable and in the arms of a man.

This was new.

Michael stayed with me for a few hours. He said he wanted to make sure I was alright but I was never going to be alright because I had too much negative baggage from my past that would always prevent me from being alright.

After taking a look at my bank statements it helped me get out of my depression and get on my grind, you see, I knew how to do that well because it was a distraction from my misery.

I spent the next few weeks picking up the pieces and one huge piece was my baby Amanda. I was thankful for Meeka taking care of her; however, my baby needed her mother.

As an apology to my clients for missing appointments, I offered them half off on their next year's taxes, and that went well. I was back, but I still had a few more people I needed to deal with, Dr. Parker, my mother, and Gary Jr.

I was determined to have a great day despite whatever happened. I checked the weather first and then I made my baby girl her favorite breakfast, waffles, and bacon before dropping her off at summer camp. Amanda loved waffles with lots of maple syrup and crisp bacon on the side.

Once we were done with breakfast, I got dressed and dressed her in the same colors I was wearing for the day; orange and yellow. Amanda loved it when we dressed alike.

Right before Amanda exited my car she looked back at me, "Mommy, have a great day okay."

I smiled and assured her I would have a great day. I had to get it together because she deserved me to be present for her. Unlike I was for her brothers, I was just there, working, and existing in a loveless marriage. I waited for her to go in and then I pulled off.

I turned on my music, Eric Benet, his music always hit the spot, and his voice relaxed me. Whenever I listened to Eric Benet I thought of Halley Berry and why such a talented and beautiful woman didn't have luck with love. Some say she's crazy, well if that's the case she and I have one thing in common.

When I pulled up at my mom's house, I took a deep breath before getting out. I saw her husband's car so I knew I had to keep it together. I rang the bell, nervous and still a little pissed that she called the police to come and check on me.

"Why hello, missy, I am glad to see you," she embraced me.

I embraced her back, a little.

"Come on in, you look pretty as always, I cooked, are you hungry?"

"No, and I can't stay long, but thanks."

"Thanks why are you acting so formal and you look stiff, what's wrong?"

God, I wanted to scream, "YOU'RE WHAT IS WRONG LADY."

"Nothing I just have a lot to do today, I wanted to stop by and let you see that I'm okay so you don't call the police again."

"I was worried, I hadn't heard from you and you," she paused, "you missed Gary J's graduation. Shana, he was hurt that you weren't there. He kept looking for you."

"Was his father there?"

"Yes, Gary was there and some new girl he's dating, and his brother and his wife came. It was nice, I really wished you would have been there, you know it's things like this, children don't ever forget."

I had to chuckle because she missed a lot of shit when we lived with our father but I guess she forgot all of that.

"Well, things happen, right?"

"You still haven't told me what happened and where were you?"

I tilted my head and I tried to focus my eyes on her to see if the concern was genuine and either my eyes were deceiving me or she was really concerned. "I'll tell you about it one day, but not today I have a lot of catching up to do."

I left her house thinking "Is it possible she forgot about my childhood?"

I called Gary J's cell phone.

"Hello Ma," he answered right away.

"Yes, it's me, your mother, where are you I'm coming to pick you up."

"I'm at work, I get off at six tonight."

I was impressed he had a job, "You have a job?"

"Yes, and a car."

Wait a minute, did he just say a car, "Your father bought you a car?"

"No, Mommom bought me a car, it's a used Camry with one hundred and ten thousand miles on it but it runs nice."

I just left her house and she never said a word about buying him a car.

"Stop by the house when you get off so I can see your new ride."

"Ma,"

"Yes,"

"I miss you and I love you and I would never do anything to embarrass you or go to prison. I got a big future ahead of me."

"I miss you too, I love you too, and that's good to know. You had me worried."

It was good to know he wasn't in prison and he was thinking like me and not his daddy.

I knew I had no business at the mall but I couldn't help myself, I wanted to treat myself to something new with a nice price tag.

I swung the door to Nordstrom open and started to look around, perfume, shoes, or a new summer outfit, I didn't know but what I did know was, I was leaving with something.

I spotted a pair of sandals by Sam Edelman,, ooh wee they were cute, and when I flipped the shoe over they were pricey but I didn't care. I sat down and looked around while I waited for a salesclerk.

I heard someone yell, "She's enjoying her life while my life is in shambles!"

I turned to my left, oh my God it was Sabian's mother.

She walked closer to me and got right up on me, "Look everyone, this is the mother of the demon that shot and killed my son."

I couldn't say anything, everyone around me was staring, my good day was starting to go bad and I would have made it worse if I had said anything. Luckily for me, security came over.

"Ma'am, is there a problem?"

She pointed at me, "Yes, this demon carrier is responsible for my son's death."

If only she knew the pain I felt for her.

The police officer looked at me and then directed his attention back to her, "Ma'am you can't do this in here, this is a business."

She started to cry, "It's not fair, it's not fair that her son gets to live, she gets to enjoy life while me and my family mourn the loss of our child."

Sam Edelman would have to wait because I had to get out of there, I got up and walked through a crowd of onlookers toward the door. I don't know why but I hate when we make a scene in front of white people. Like, do we really need to impress the evilest of all races?

I got to my car and closed my eyes for a few minutes, not even Eric Benet could soothe me out of this but I was not going to fall into a rabbit hole again, but did she call me a demon carrier.

Dr. Parker's office

After the shenanigans at the mall, I threw myself onto Dr. Parkers Couch.

"I was worried about you Shana, you haven't picked up your prescriptions from the pharmacy and you missed our last appointment, what has been going on?"

I fell into a deep depression, and I couldn't find my way out. It reminded me of when Gary's family moved to Georgia and moved in with us. He dismissed my feelings and tried to make me feel low when they were around. He tried to make me look dumb and I might be a lot of things but dumb is not one of them.

I started noticing that Gary was treating me differently when his family was around, and they would treat me differently too. I felt disrespected by his family, especially his mom but his dad loved me. He didn't have a great relationship with his mother and he barely knew his father. I think his father was a rolling stone, and Gary's mother got rolled over twice because Gary's brother was the apple of her eye.

I watched Gary try to impress her, please her, and nothing he did make her look at him the same way she looked at his brother, I felt a little bad for him.

He would let his family eat, sleep and drink and not charge them a dime and I was the one carrying all of the weight. He made it seem like he was paying for the house, cars, and clothes but it was me. Every single time his family came to visit, we would get into an argument because he let them run our household and when I tried to stand up he would fight with me.

Gary always told me, "Family Over Everything FOE and he didn't mean me and our family. He and his family had FOE tattooed on their body. I always felt like an outsider whenever around his family; I never felt like I was important to him and the crazy part was I always made him feel secure. Everyone knew he was important to me even though my family and friends saw him do some shady shit.

The only time he ever had my back was when my father tried to sue me.

"Why did your father try to sue you, Shana?"

"Oh my goodness, I didn't tell you about that."

In 2014, As I've told you, my father got into the tax business after he came out of rehab he had several offices. My father was always great with numbers and making money but he went too far and got caught. Unbeknown to me he was lying on people's taxes and the IRS caught up with him. He never thought he would go to prison, so on the day of court he showed up in a suit, drove his Bentley, and told his family he would see them in a few hours.

I was the only one that showed up in court for him, his wife nor his other children went.

Well, he got a rude awakening because the female judge laid him out in the courtroom and told him he was arrogant and a narcissist.

When she gave him ten years for tax fraud, my jaw dropped along with tears, I was not prepared for my dad to go to prison. I cried in the courtroom like a little girl, and he never turned to look at me, I know he heard me crying but he never acknowledged me.

My father never broke down, humbled himself, or anything, he just looked straight ahead with no emotion.

"Your father and Gary have a lot in common when it comes to acknowledging your pain."

I walked out of the courtroom and sat in my car thinking "What am I going to do?"

A few hours later he was allowed to make a phone call and he called me. I was so happy to hear his voice, that's until he told me to make sure I keep his business and to make sure I take care of his wife and children, he wanted me to pay his mortgage and his cars. It was my responsibility to make sure his family was taken care of with his business.

He didn't care about me my siblings or my children, but I kept quiet and listened, and everything he told me to do I was going to do it.

I worked my ass off during tax time and I paid his mortgage for the year, his cars, and made sure his wife and kids had money. Sometimes I didn't have enough for my family but I didn't care.

That's until Liberty taxes came knocking at my door because it was time to renew contracts for them. I went over the contracts and found out my father lied to me; he didn't own the clients, nor the program system, he was renting everything from Liberty.

Therefore I didn't owe him a dime and I was busting my ass for him, putting money on his books, and I kept his wife in Chanel while I was shopping at the swap meet for me and my children. I was furious.

I wrote him a letter and told him I would no longer be taking care of his family and I told him why.

Liberty Taxes told me I could start my own franchise and that's what me and Gary did.

The next year I was up and running four tax stores.

My father was furious and threatened to sue me, and he attempted to however he didn't have a leg to stand on. I held all of the cards and it felt good but that didn't stop him, he continued suing me and he and his wife were demanding a settlement.

His wife contacted me telling me they were struggling and she was going to lose the house, she even threatened me and tried to steal my clients.

I was pregnant with Amanda while my father was suing me and I was tired of fighting in court.

I told my lawyer to pay him one hundred thousand dollars and that was my final offer.

He took the money but he wrote me again and told me he wasn't done with me and he was going to put me and my family in the poor house.

The funny part was he was fighting with me and going blind at the same time. That's narcissism for you.

"Why was he going blind, Shana?"

"He was a diabetic and he lost his eyesight but that didn't stop his evilness, he continued suing just like he said he would.

"Is he still blind?"

"No, I heard he can see again."

"Shana we went over a lot today and I'm starting to see that you suppress your true feelings and that will keep you depressed. You don't have to curse people out or get indignant however you do need to teach people how to treat you."

"I hear you Dr. Parker and I'm trying; I didn't tell you Gary Sr. called the police on me last month."

Dr. Parker shook her head, "what happened?" She looked at her watch just as was about to tell her.

"Wait, let's continue on Friday."

"You want me to come back twice in a week?"

"Yes Shana, we need more sessions."

When I left therapy my cell phone rang and it was one of my clients from Georgia, Aston. Aston had a big crush on me and he let it be known after Gary and I divorced but I couldn't take him seriously because he told me he was divorced, and then I met his ex-wife and she said they were working on getting back together.

I didn't have any rap for him on a relationship level but I kept him as a friend.

"Hey Aston, what's going on?" His Jamaican accent turned me on.

"Hey baby girl, how are you, I miss you being in Georgia, come back to me."

I laughed, "I might come and visit but I'm in Delaware to stay."

"Oh baby, it's nothing there for you but cold weather."

"Aston, what's up what can I do for you?"

"I was thinking about you and I'm going home to Jamaica for a week and I want you to come with me."

"I have a child you know."

"Bring her along, I will welcome her."

"Let me look at my schedule and get back to you." I knew I was not going with him.

"Okay let me know, beautiful."

Island men make American women feel wanted.

Another call to interrupt my thoughts, "Hello,"

"Hello Mrs. Cole, this is Baltimore City supermax prison."

"Yes, what's wrong with Wendell!" my heart was pounding.

"Your son was attacked by another inmate in the shower."

I panicked, "where is he now?"

"He's at the University of Maryland however you can't see him."

"that's bullshit, I want to see my son!"

"Ma'am you'll have to take that up with the warden of the prison."

"Connect me," I waited on hold for twenty minutes, and then I hung up.

I took a deep breath, why was it that every time I left therapy I dealt with bullshit.

CHAPTER EIGHT

I dropped Amanda off at Meeka's and flew to Baltimore, I tried anyway because the 95-south traffic from Delaware to Baltimore is hell at five in the afternoon.

Once arrived at the hospital I was told to go to shock Trauma, I knew then it wasn't good. I walked a long scary hallway, I felt like I was in a horror movie walking down the hallway.

I saw two officers standing guard, I walked right up to them and told them who I was and that I wanted to see my son. They both stopped me and told me I could not go in but I could, however, look through the window at him.

I pitched a fit, I was his mother and I wanted to see my son, but they would not let me go in. I walked over to the window and there he was lying in the bed with tubes helping him hang on to life. I dropped my head and began to pray; was I wrong to feel for a split second "Why would God want to save him?"

Flashes of him as a baby appeared, he was my firstborn child and the first love of my life. I started hyperventilating again so I found a place to sit and wait for the doctors.

Hours had gone by, so I needed to call Meeka and let her know that I would come in the morning to get Amanda. She assured me that Amanda was okay and to take as much time as I needed.

I had fallen asleep in the chair, and then around three o'clock in the morning, I woke up to screaming and chaos. I jumped up and saw the officers trying to restrain him through the window and before I knew it I attempted to run into the room.

One of the officers tried to hold me back and that infuriated Wendell, he started yelling "Let my mother go, get your hands off of my mother!"

Wendell was too much for one officer so he called for backup and the next thing I saw was ten to twelve officers coming through the door. I was scared for my son.

I pleaded with the officers, "Just let me talk to him, please."

The officer felt sorry for me; I saw it in his eyes. He must be a momma's boy and he felt my pain.

"Okay, but be brief and we will be standing right here with you.

The other officers didn't like it at all.

I walked over to his bed and leaned over, "Son, what happened to you, who did this to you and why?"

He stared into my eyes like a little boy.

"Wendell, if you can hear me I need you to nod."

Instead of nodding, he looked away from me.

I grew angry and started yelling, "Tell me what did I do to make you this, this monster. I don't even know you. I didn't raise you to be like this. What the fuck did I do to deserve this!" I lost it, I needed answers, answers that he never gave me.

I got his attention, and he turned and looked at me, he opened his eyes and I saw tears in his eyes.

"Say something, please, Wendell."

He motioned for me to lean closer to him so I did and he whispered in my ear.

For five minutes I was in shock and stunned and then I grew angry. I couldn't believe what he told me.

He looked away again so I grabbed him and that's when the officers grabbed me by the arm and told me I had to leave.

I yanked my arm from him and told him I wasn't ready yet.

"Ma'am let's go, you can leave walking handcuffed or not but you're leaving now."

He was a big white tall officer and I was mad but not stupid so I left to keep him from putting his hands on me.

I was in a daze and the ride back to Delaware was foggy, my head was all messed up. I couldn't put it together but I was going to.

I called Meeka and told her I needed her to keep Amanda overnight again. I needed to think and process everything and I didn't need any distractions.

I forgot I needed money for the Delaware toll, which meant I was going to get a big fine for not having four dollars but that was the least of my worries.

I had to pee like a racehorse so I stopped at McDonald's but they weren't open yet. I could feel the pee coming and I didn't want to pee on my leather seats, I had no choice but to squat down next to my car and pee; it was such a relief to pee.

I pulled up to the front of my house at exactly four o'clock in the morning and to my surprise, I saw Gary J's car parked in my driveway and he was sitting on my steps.

He ran to my car.

"What's wrong, why are you here, is everything okay?"

"My dad put me out and I need to move back home."

I sat there a few more seconds and prayed, "Lord, step in because I'm on autopilot and I need your guidance."

I stepped out of my car and walked around the car and walked to the house, I ignored him.

"Ma, please I don't have any place to go!"

I snapped because he raised his voice, my prayer for patience was mute at this point.

"You moved out to go and live with your father, you gave me a long speech about how wonderful it would be and all the freedom you were going to have. So go back to your freedom."

"When I open this door, I have things I need to take care of and I don't need any distractions."

He stood there looking stupid as I opened the door. "Ma, I need you can you please be here for me for once, damn!"

I turned around faster than a white cop pulling over a black man driving a BMW, "Don't curse at me, are you crazy?"

I saw his frustration but still, he was wrong.

"I'm sorry, it's just that I feel like you don't."

He stopped talking.

"I don't what, tell me," Now I was frustrated.

"You don't love me because my father is an ass hole."

Was he for real or was he being like his father a manipulator, I couldn't tell.

"I love you however lately you've been acting differently which is causing us to bump heads and as far as your father is concerned how I feel about him has no bearing on my love for my children."

As I was talking I realized, yeah he is full of shit because Amanda is Gary's child and he didn't include her. This is what I don't have time for, GAMES and I thought to myself, "I'm not going to entertain it for a second."

He pleaded, "Ma, I'm homeless, please let me move back in."

I stared at him for a moment, unable to say anything and I thought about the consequences of closing the door in his face. I would essentially be throwing my child onto the streets and whatever the streets had to offer him.

"Come on in but leave your bags out there," I was stern.

I walked into the living room, "have a seat."

He sat down like a little puppy dog, humble.

I remained standing, I needed him to know I was serious, "I have rules in this house and if you want to stay here until you go to college you will follow them or you will be put out of this house. Do I make myself clear?"

"Yes ma'am,"

"I am serious, I don't want girls in my house when I'm not home, your curfew is two a.m. and you have to save money for college."

"Yes ma'am."

He would say anything to get his way just like his father.

"Okay go and get your stuff but remember my house my rules."

I don't know what happened at Gary's house and I didn't give a damn.

My mind wandered back to Wendell, I needed to get to the bottom of what he told me.

I decided to see if Gary J knew anything, "Hey, did you and your brother ever talk about his childhood?"

"No, Wendell was quiet, ma, you know that."

I talked with my hands hoping he would catch on, "Did he ever tell you personal stuff about himself?"

"Nope, never," he shook his head.

"Are you sure he never said anything to you about having sex with anybody?"

"Ma, we never talked about sex, we barely talked to each other. He's my brother and I love him but he was strange."

"Strange, strange how?"

"Things like going in the bathroom to shower fully dressed and coming out of the bathroom completely dressed. He would barricade the bathroom door every time he went to the bathroom and every time I walked into the room with a towel around me he would immediately leave."

Gary J hunched his shoulders, "I thought it was weird like one-time Dad walked into the bathroom while he was in the shower and Wendell had on a t-shirt and shorts taking a shower. He was special."

How did I miss all of that?

Gary J went upstairs to his bedroom while I sat in the kitchen staring out of the window watching the sun come up, it was going to be a hot summer day but not hotter than I was. I didn't know how to process everything.

Gary J left for work around eight a.m. and I was still sitting, thinking. That's when I received the call.

"May I speak with Shanna Cole?"

"Yes, this is Shanna Cole."

"Ms. Cole this is Warden Simpson, I'm sorry ma'am, I have bad news. Your son Wendell died at seven-thirty a.m. this morning. The doctors did everything they could to help him.

I dropped the phone, and the room began to spin, I kept hearing the words dead, dead, dead over and over again.

I survived being raised by a crackhead father, having no electricity for years, going weeks without food in my belly, being teased because I didn't look like the other kids in school, being abandoned by my mother, having a cheating drug addict husband, and a murderer son but standing over my son's coffin and watching it lowered into a grave was harder than anything I have ever gone through.

Wendell Sr. hadn't seen his son in years but he got clean enough to attend his funeral along with some other of his relatives.

The rip between my father and I was so tattered that he didn't feel the need to attend his grandson's funeral nor send his condolences, but I wasn't surprised. His narcissism would allow him to show compassion for me.

Gary stepped up and was there for his children and I appreciated him for that.

I couldn't wait to get to therapy. I needed someone to help me process everything.

Dr. Parker, I missed the signs, I was so busy making a life for myself, the life that I laid awake at night as a child and imagined; I forgot my children's lives. I was selfish and now I am paying for it.

I worked my ass off to give, and to give and to give some more because nobody gave me when I was a child, no love, no understanding, no time, nothing! I thought by giving I would be blessed what happened to my blessing, did God forget me!

I need answers, God needs to answer me because this therapy thing it's not working. I'm worse than when I started. My life is falling apart and I don't know how to recover.

"Dr. Parker, are you listening to me!"

Dr. Parker uncrossed her legs and leaned toward me, "Shanna, I am listening to you and I am here to help you process everything that's going on. Your anger is understandable; however, you need to take the prescription I gave you and schedule more therapy sessions."

"Why, I'm giving you the bits and pieces of my life and what am I getting in return, replaying my pain it's making it worse" I couldn't stop crying. "I need to put this therapy on pause and I'm not taking medication and that's period."

I left her office with no intention of ever going back; I was on a mission to clear my son's name and nothing was going to stop me.

CHAPTER NINE

It Can't Rain Forever

Two months later, I was worse than before, I couldn't sleep, I didn't know who I was but I did know how to work and make money. That was my therapy.

Sabian's family rejoiced at Wendell's death and they went on every media outlet talking about their son and how my son got what he deserved. However, Gary told me the streets were talking and it was a prison hit by Sabian's father, Gill.

I didn't tell anyone what Wendell whispered to me but I knew I had to let my son's pain be heard but I needed to do some investigating first.

Gary J left for Howard University and I couldn't be prouder of my son, I gave a going away dinner for him and my family and Gary's family showed up and out. We sent him off with money, prayers, and condoms. I told him not to call me and tell me "Ma she is pregnant."

It was me and Amanda in the house and it got lonely some days and nights but I occupied my time with work, motherhood, and being a detective.

Gary did step up, I guess he felt something for me, his child support checks were coming regularly and he paid me back the money took from me. Amanda liked his girlfriend and she spent a lot of time with them and her daughter.

I was becoming an empty nester, something I had dreamed about but never imagined. I had never lived alone; I had been a mother since I was fifteen. I went from living as a child to being a woman and parent. This was strange territory.

Meeka called me Friday morning and invited me out with her, her sister, and their friends to Downtown Delaware to see Carl Thomas; she knew he was my favorite artist.

I told her I was busy but she wasn't taking no for an answer; besides she knew I didn't have plans on a Friday night and she knew I needed a distraction. I gave in and agreed to hang out with them.

I looked through my closet, and then at my hair, I didn't have a clue as to what to wear, I hadn't been out in years and I haven't had my hair done in months. I had to get it together so I didn't embarrass myself or my friend.

I was nervous about going out until I looked in the mirror, I looked good, no scratch that, I looked damn good with my skinny ripped jeans, Jessica Simpson red pumps, white tank top, and multicolored J Crew linen blazer. The hair was easy, and my natural look never failed.

I pulled up at the spot, parked, and stepped looking like I didn't have a care in the world, if only that were true. I walked up to the front of the club and was immediately greeted.

"Hello, beautiful stranger, this is a wonderful surprise, I think about you from time to time."

I could not say the same but it was nice to know someone was thinking about me.

"Hello, Michael."

"Are you alone or meeting someone?"

"I'm meeting some girlfriends here for the show."

"Well as you can see, I'm working tonight so I will be sure to keep you safe."

I blushed, "thank you."

Meeka and the others were walking toward me, we all hugged and greeted each other and then walked off. I turned around and glanced back at Michael and to my surprise he was watching me.

Meeka doesn't miss a thing she picked up on it, "What's with you and the officer?"

"That's the police officer I was telling you about."

"Owe that's Michael, hmmm, he looks good. I think you need to consider him."

"Girl let's enjoy this show because I don't know when I'm going to come out again.

The show was off the hook and I was having drinks and shots, and when Carl Thomas came out I lost my mind. I sang every song along with him, and the crowd was pumped up.

It was my turn to go and get drinks; it was going to be hard to carry the drinks with the heels I had on but I attempted it. I walked up to the bar and I happened to see Michael standing to my right. It's amazing how alcohol will make you bold.

I walked up to him, "Excuse me are you busy."

He looked down at me and smiled, "You have been drinking young lady."

"Yes, and I'm going to need an escort home, officer."

"Well, I'll make sure you get one."

I smiled back at him, "Thank you, officer." I was smashed for sure.

After the show was over, it was clear to Meeka that I could not drive myself home and I couldn't leave my car at the garage overnight or I would have a two hundred dollar bill the next day but I couldn't risk driving home.

Meeka damn near carried me to her car, "You had a great time didn't you."

I hugged her and tears formed in my eyes, "Thank you, thank you for always being there for me and never wanting anything in return. You are more of a sister to me than my own sister."

I could tell she was getting emotional too and it was all good.

It was a knock on her driver's window and it scared the shit out of both of us, we jumped.

"Excuse me,"

It was Michael, Meeka rolled down the window.

"I'm off duty and I can take her home."

Meeka looked at him as if to say, "Are you crazy."

Michael got the message, "I'm sorry if I overstepped."

He was big overstepping, we always had a rule, we came together and we left together and that wasn't going to change.

Meeka checked him right away, "I got this, I'll take her home." We pulled off and I looked out of the side mirror and saw him watching as we drove away.

"He wants you."

"Yeah, you think?"

I fell asleep as soon as we got on the highway and all I remembered when we pulled up in front of my house was Carl Thomas singing to me.

Meeka walked me to the door and made sure I was in the house safe and then she left.

I took my clothes off and went straight to bed. The next morning

God, I had the worst headache when I got up to go to the bathroom. I peed like I had drunk a brewery. On my way back to my bed I peeped outside and I panicked, "Where was my car, somebody had stolen my car!"

I grabbed my cell phone to call Meeka and that's when it hit me, my car was still at the parking garage. I was in a dilemma, I needed someone to come to pick me up and take me to my car. I couldn't ask Meeka, or should I say I didn't want to, I had to respect her husband.

I decided to call Michael and ask him, I was nervous.

"Hello, Michael this is Shanna, how are you?"

"I am good I was going to call you today but I figured I would let you sleep in, you had quite a night."

"Yes, I did," I was silent for a minute, "Michael would you do me a big favor, I left my car at the club garage and I don't have any way to get there. A lift would cost me way too much."

"Sure, I'm off today, how about I come pick you up and we maybe we can go to lunch."

"Okay, I like that, you know where I live already," I laughed.

"Yes, I do in Middletown; I'm on my way."

I hopped in the shower to rinse last night off of me. As the water beat down on me my thoughts turned to Wendell, I felt guilty about enjoying myself knowing my son was taken from me not just in death but in life. I was tired of crying but that's what depression and anxiety do to you.

I hadn't been on a date in so long that I forgot what to wear to look cute, but I thought, it's Saturday, and we're only going to lunch so I threw on a pair of black leggings, my black and red Jordan sneakers, a red t-shirt and grabbed my coach backpack. I kept it simple.

I went downstairs to wait for Michael to pull up and while I was waiting Gary Sr. called to say he needed to drop Amanda off. It's just like him to do something like this, I think he has a radar on my life. I had to cancel my plans.

I waited for Gary to pull up to drop Amanda off, hoping he would come before Michael.

Twenty minutes later Michael and Gary pulled up at the same time.

Gary looked at Michael but didn't speak, however, Michael spoke to him.

Amanda runs to me, "Mommy, I had a good time with Daddy."

Gary looked over at Michael, "Who is that nigga?"

Are my ears failing me, I thought he asked me a question that was none of his damn business, so I ignored him.

"Shanna, who is that?"

"None of your business, Gary"

"Is this your man?" He's caught an attitude.

"Bye, I have to go," I came out of the house, locked the door, and grabbed Amanda by her hand, "We are hanging out today."

Michael walked up to meet me, he smiled at Amanda, "Hi,"

"Shanna, don't ignore me!"

But I did, "I'm sorry about lunch my daughter just got dropped off."

"She can go with us; I don't have a problem with that."

"Okay, let's go." We walked to his car, and he opened the door for Amanda and me.

We left Gary standing on the sidewalk looking stupid.

"Bye Daddy, see you next week." Amanda waved to him.

I chuckled inside, it felt good to see him looking lost.

Michael pulled up to Chuckie Cheese and parked. I looked at him, dude this is not where I want to eat.

He caught my vibe without me saying a word, "What, you don't like Chuckie?"

Amanda was in the back of the car excited.

Michael got out of the car and opened my door and Amanda's door; I didn't expect anything less.

While Amanda played he and I talked, it was refreshing to talk to a man with aspirations. He told me what he wanted for his future and we laughed at the children playing. He and I played games and won Amanda tickets. Before I knew it I was enjoying myself and it felt good to laugh and think about something else.

We were in Chuckie Cheese for three hours it felt like thirty minutes because time got away from us.

Michael took me to my car; we pulled up to the attendant and my bill was two hundred dollars for leaving my car overnight but Michael said something to the attendant and showed his badge and I ended up paying twenty dollars.

I was grateful for that because I did not have two hundred dollars to spare this time or any other time.

I offered Michael dinner if he followed me home and thought maybe we could have some drinks after dinner. I wanted to show my gratitude.

He excepted and followed me to my house.

I whipped up something simple and the three of us sat at the dining room table and ate, laughed, and had a good time.

It was getting late and I was tired, I needed to put Amanda to bed so it was time for Michael to leave. I walked him to the door and thanked him again for all of his help.

"You are a beautiful, intelligent, and funny lady. I hope this is not our last date."

"No not at all and I had a great time."

I didn't know if I should kiss him or not but he settled that by leaning towards me and planting a big kiss on my cheek.

That was a great ending to a great day I thought to myself.

Michael and I started spending a lot of time talking on the phone while he was on duty and every now and then I would meet him for lunch and take him food, he loved my peach cobbler. I wasn't sure if we were making a connection outside of the friend zone. It had been a very long time since I had been intimate with a man but I didn't forget what needed to be done to get the job done.

Every time I was in his presence he made me feel sexy even when I would show up wearing sweats and flip-flops.

Michael told me he had some vacation time coming up in October and he wanted to go away. He wanted to know if my schedule was clear to go but first, he wanted me to meet his family. I was wondering when that was going to happen because I don't get serious with a man until I meet his circle.

He planned our date for a Sunday and we went to his mom's house where I met her, his dad, and his two sisters. Everyone was nice and made me feel right at home, it felt their strength as a family.

After meeting his family I agreed to go away with him. I worked for myself so clearing my schedule was not a problem, however, I did need a babysitter for Amanda and it could not be Gary's nosey ass.

I reached out to my mother and Meeka and both of them were more than happy to take care of Amanda for a week. I was excited, I had never been on a vacation that I didn't pay for so this was a first but I didn't know where we were going.

Michael asked me to go on vacation with him to the Bahamas, I had never been out of the United States so I was game to go.

I started thinking, I really don't know this man like that and I've watched a lot of 48 hours and I wasn't trying to be the next episode.

I decided to throw a card party and I invited, Meeka, Reginald, my aunts, and cousins. I wanted everyone to meet Michael just in case I didn't make it back from the Bahamas.

I introduced Michael to my family and they loved him, which I knew they would, and he surprised me by being the life of the party.

Michael stayed and helped me clean up after everyone had left; Amanda went to bed hours ago so it was just us talking and laughing about the night.

Up until now we hadn't had much touch and feeling, it was always a kiss on the lips occasionally. I don't know what he was waiting for because I wanted to fuck the shit out of him. Just looking at his tall fine, muscle-built ass made me cum but I was a lady and kept my legs close. My rose got a serious work out though and it wasn't getting the job done anymore.

We were in the kitchen washing and drying dishes when he turned and kissed me, I mean really kissed me, "Oh shit, this is it," I thought to myself.

After the kiss he stepped back, "Is it okay if I crash in your guest room, I am in no shape to drive."

The guest room is this man for real, "sure" I shook my head.

"Thank you I wouldn't want to get pulled over."

We both laughed, but he was serious after all he is a black man before he is a black cop to a white state trooper.

I went upstairs and fixed up the guest room with clean sheets and made sure he would be comfortable. He came up behind me and placed his arms around my waist, "will you be joining me in the guest room?"

I turned and looked at him puzzled.

"I don't want to be with you in your bed, I want to be with you in a bed you have never slept in."

How does he know I've never slept in this bed? "How do you know I haven't?"

"Have you," he asked while rubbing my ass and kissing my neck.

I was melting like a chocolate candy bar left in a hot car, or vanilla ice cream in a microwave.

"No, I have never slept in this bed."

"You see I knew that."

He closed the door and we started undressing each other, clothes were flying everywhere. I could not wait to fuck him and apparently, he felt the same way, but we had to keep it quiet because my daughter was upstairs.

This is what my body was craving, it was a high I didn't want to come down from. The orgasms were exploding from my inner being and I felt my heart beating as he fucked me. I was so selfish I could not think about pleasing him, it was all about me and somehow he sensed that.

The thrust, flipping me all around had me moaning and calling his name over and over and then he opened his mouth and said, "suck my dick."

"What," You know what, fuck it, I'm sucking his dick and it was a big one. I wrapped my lips around his dick and took it straight to the back of my mouth. He definitely felt my tonsils and then I waited for him to lose his mind.

He moaned louder than I did, toes curled and all, but to my surprise he was not done with me. We went from aggressive sex to making love and that was messing with my head. I didn't stop him instead I let him make love to me until we both exploded.

I snuggled in his arms, it felt like a dream, and I didn't want to wake up.

The sun was coming up and I could see it through the blinds, I looked into Michael's face and he looked like a happy man. I tried to ease out of his arms but he pulled me close to him.

"Don't leave me," he said.

"I have to get up for Amanda, she needs breakfast."

"Okay," he says right before his cell phone rang.

It was different than I had heard before, my antenna went up. That's what happens when you get great sex you become anxious he does about everything. I never liked that part.

"It's my job calling; there's a shooter at Walmart!" He jumped out of bed and got dressed.

"You have to go, where is your stuff to shoot back."

"Everything I need is in my car in the glove compartment, my gun and my badge and my vest is in the trunk of my car.

Oh no I don't like this part, and then it hit me, "dammit, he's a police officer."

I got nervous and turned on the news and it was breaking news all over the place. Wait that's the Walmart up the street from me. "Please be safe and careful," I said right before he went out of the door.

He kissed me and ran to his car.

I cooked breakfast for me and Amanda but I couldn't eat my nerves were all over the place. I was watching the television and they reported nine people were shot and two of them were police officers.

I was pacing, the floor and looking at my cell phone, "Ring, call me Michael call me."

At that moment I knew I was not cut out to be with a police officer.

I went to my office and worked on a few clients' accounts to take my mind off of Michael and it was working. Work was always my distraction from problems, people, and things. It got me thinking is this how I missed the signs of Wendell's trauma.

It was after five o'clock and I still hadn't heard from Michael, I tried to control my thoughts but it was hard. I had so many hypotheticals racing through my mind.

I put Amanda to bed around eight o'clock and then I took a gummy to relax me so I could fall asleep and that's just what I did and that's when the phone rang; it was Michael.

I answered with haste, "Michael are you alright?"

"Yes, I'm fine, I had a lot of paperwork to do but I'm good. We got the bad guy."

I took a sigh of relief.

"Are you alright, you sound worked up?"

I didn't want to admit it to him, "I was nervous, I was worried about you."

"Babe, this is the life of a police officer. Remember you asked me why I wasn't in a relationship, well here's why. It's dangerous and we get calls to show up when the bad guys act up."

I didn't hear anything after babe, him calling me babe was so sweet.

"Are you sure you want to go down this road?"

"Yes, I'm sure," I wanted to sound convincing however I was lying.

"I'll see you tomorrow, I need to tie up some loose ends."

I sighed and then immediately called Meeka, I had to tell somebody, anybody about how this man fucked me right.

CHAPTER TEN

It's More to It

One week before the Bahamas

I stopped keeping my appointments with Dr. Parker, she called but I swiped left and sent her straight to voicemail. I had something positive in my life and I didn't want to be reminded of past hurt and disappointments.

I finally got up the nerve to tell Wendell Sr. what our son told me Gill did to him and he looked at me as if he had seen a ghost.

He did see a ghost, Wendell Sr. burst into tears and confessed that Wendell Jr. came to him the day before he killed Sabian and told him Gill molested him and he didn't believe him.

He said he thought Wendell Jr. was lying because he and Gill ran the streets together back in the day. Wendell Sr. is the one who recommended we take our son to Gill's mother's daycare.

Wendell Sr. was sobbing and torn after I told him.

Word on the street was Wendell went to rehab again to get clean. Only God knows if it's going to work this time. I always wanted Wendell to get his life together for himself and Wendell. However, our son was gone and I didn't care anymore.

I planned my attack strategically by contacting a content creator with a YouTube channel called Shame the Devil and that's what I wanted to do.

Shame the Devil channeled outed child molesters; people called in and talked about the people who molested them and today was my day. I'm not going to lie I was nervous but I was on a mission.

I sat my laptop up in my office and I was ready for my seven o'clock Zoom call. I tried to rehearse what I was going to say but at the last minute, I decided to just flow with it.

It was seven o'clock on the dot when she zoomed me in

"Hello Shanna, welcome to Shame the Devil, say hello to the audience.

"Hello," I waved.

"Okay we have five hundred people watching the interview so let's get started. First, tell everyone how you found the channel and then why you reached out to me.

"I was trolling through YouTube and stumbled on it, I wasn't looking for anything in particular. I saw your catchphrase and I was intrigued by the stories and the comments, I listened to all of your segments and I knew I needed to tell my son's story."

"Tell us your story, Shanna."

I took a deep breath and began to tell his story, "My son Wendell started changing when he was around nine years old, he would steal from stores, act out in school, and fight all the time and I thought it was a phase he was going through however when he got older he didn't change. I would whoop him, punish him but nothing seemed to faze him. He didn't show any love or care for his siblings."

"What about his relationship with you, you know a son's first love is his mother?"

A lump formed in my throat, "Because of my childhood I wasn't very affectionate, meaning I didn't hug, or say I love you a lot. I showed my love by giving." I paused because I didn't know what else to say.

"Okay go on, and just so you know, this is a no-judgment zone, okay."

Thank God she said that, but people say that but they still judge, "Okay," I told her.

"Wendell Jr. would fight a lot in school, but I thought it was because we were new in Atlanta from Delaware and you know how kids can be cruel if you talk differently or dress differently so I dismissed it. I know now I should not have.

Wendell Jr. and my ex-husband didn't get along at all, my son would walk around the house and avoid my husband."

"Was your ex-husband his father?"

"No, he is the father to my other two children."

"Where was Wendell Jr's father?"

"That's another story for another session."

I was becoming uncomfortable, and I was hoping she would notice.

"Okay, go on, Shanna."

"I was working a lot with my father trying to build the family business so my ex-husband took care of Wendell Jr. a lot of the time."

"Excuse me, I don't mean to interrupt you, but how did your ex-husband treat Wendell Jr was he loving to him, did he act like his biological dad or did he act like a stepdad?"

She just confused the hell out of me, "To be honest I can't say, all I know is they bumped heads here and there and I assumed it was because Wendell Jr. was growing up and smelling himself. Gary did correct him from time to time."

I continued, "Fast forward, things started falling apart with my marriage after I had my daughter, and I packed up my children, filed for a divorce, and moved back to Delaware. I thought things would get better for Wendell Jr. because he could connect with his father and his side of the family but it did not."

"Why, what was going on with his father?"

I stared at the computer before I answered her. Why did this feel like a session with Dr. Parker?

"Wendell's father was an addict and he didn't care about Wendell." I continued, "Wendell didn't want to go to school so he dropped out and things got worse. The police were always calling me at work, and no matter what I did or said to Wendell Jr. things never got better."

Now here comes the hard part and I had to remember we were live and people were listening, "A year after moving to Delaware, Wendell Jr. decided to go and visit his father in Southbridge, I don't know what happened when he got there, but I didn't see or hear from my son after that. The next time I saw him it was on the eleven o'clock news, he was wanted for murder."

I saw the gasp and the look on her face I didn't know if should I go on or not so I stopped.

"Go on, I'm listening," she said.

"I was shocked and just stunned, my son killed someone, I didn't know the person I saw on TV, I mean I knew him but that wasn't my son. My son was tried and convicted and sentenced to life in prison, but it didn't stop there. He escaped from the courthouse and well let's just say things went from worse to unbelievable. Two months ago Wendell Jr. was stabbed in prison and when I went to see him he told me for the first time why he killed the fifteen-year-old boy."

"Why, why," she looked anxious for an answer.

"He told me that Sabian's father, Gill Knight molested him when he was a little boy and that's why he killed Sabian."

Tru-Tea put her hand over her mouth, "Oh my goodness."

She was just as shocked as I was.

I went on to tell the story, "Sabian's grandmother Joyce ran a daycare center for many years, and un-be-knowing to the parents her son was a predator. My son told me before he died that Gill use to touch him and the other kids. He used to line them up and put his dick in their mouth and inside of them.

"Oh my goodness I am so sorry," Ms. Tru Tea was in tears.

I started to cry, "My son told me that he killed Sabian to get back at his father for raping him! My son was murdered in prison, and some people listening might say he got what he deserved but he lived with pain all those years and I didn't know!" I was an emotional wreck and I didn't care. I wanted the whole world to hear my son's pain.

"Shanna I typically open the phones up for questions however, I can't right now, but what I will do is post this on YouTube right away."

"Thank you Ms. Tru-Tea for having me, and I hope this video helps somebody."

I logged off the Zoom call and attempted to work the rest of the day but I couldn't my spirit was too shaken.

Later in the day, I pulled myself off of the sofa, cooked dinner for Amanda, and went to pick her up from school.

Watching my baby run to my car put a smile on my face and I needed her to know that because I have been preoccupied with my thoughts.

Weeks leading up to our vacation Michael was super busy, I didn't realize it was that much crime in Delaware but that wasn't all that was happening.

Apparently, my interview with Ms. Tru-Tea was spreading and everyone was talking about it.

I looked online and just about every blogger had a caption about my interview and that's just what I wanted.

Bahamas here I come!

The night before we were to leave I dropped Amanda off at my mom's house and I went to Michael's house to stay. It felt good to be at Michael's house, his house smelled good, it was clean and he had exquisite taste in furniture.

My bags were packed with sexy bathing suits and basically, that was it. I didn't plan to wear much else of anything, well, I did buy some sexy negligees to make sure I had Michael's attention the entire vacation.

Michael and I boarded the plane, I screamed inside my head, "I'm going to the Bahamas!" and then I turned to Michael and smiled. If only he knew how happy I was.

After the plane landed we checked into a villa, not a hotel and it was breathtakingly beautiful; he planned the perfect trip.

I noticed Micheal was unusually quiet the entire flight and after we landed. I was curious but I didn't want to annoy him with questions, however, my mind was all over the place.

I thought I did something, I said something, and he doesn't like me anymore. I didn't know what to think and I couldn't turn the voices in my head to stop talking to me.

Michael planned a couple's massage for us, and I was excited about it and I hoped the massage helped him to open up about what was going on. His silence was killing me softly.

We were facing each other during the massage, I opened my eyes and looked over at him but his eyes were closed. I stared into his face, thinking to myself, what have a done? I was so gripped by my thoughts to enjoy the massage.

After the massages, we sat by the pool, my abs were tight and my ass looked perfect; after all, I spent weeks working out and it definitely paid off. I wanted to tantalize him with my sexy two-piece bathing suit and prayed it worked.

Michael's sexy body screamed, "I'm sexy and I know it." I looked over at him, wearing dark sunshades, and aqua-blue swim trunks.

We were relaxing and taking in the sun.

"I heard your interview with Tru-tea."

I leaned forward from the chair, I never told Michael about Wendell, "Oh, okay."

"Why didn't you tell me about your son." He continued looking straight ahead.

"I swung my legs around and faced him, "You want to talk about it now?"

"Yes," he lifted his sunshades and faced me.

"My son was incarcerated for murder, he died a few months ago and before he died he told me he was molested by the father of the person he killed."

After I got it all out, I waited for his response.

"I'm sorry for your loss," he leaned over and hugged me.

"Thank you," I didn't know what else to say. Could this have been what was bothering him?"

He jumped into the pool, "Come on and get in."

I took off my sarong and walked into the warm water.

"Do you know how to swim," he asked.

"No, but I can float." I was holding onto the side of the pool for dear life.

"Come on I got you," Michael held his arms out.

Other people were in the pool, and we joined them and played volleyball. After the sun had set we had an intimate dinner and retired back to our room and slept.

I woke up the next morning feeling cheated because I thought he would be all over me, but instead, I slept in his arms.

The rest of the vacation was fun-filled with no thrills.

Back from vacation and entering chaos.

Sabian's mother Loraine was out for blood and it was my blood because the backlash from my interview on YouTube was crazy so crazy that Loraine sent me a letter to cease and desist spreading lies and rumors about her husband.

What Loraine didn't know was I was just getting started because I believed my son. He was dead but his truth was going to be told.

My social media was crazy, some people were attacking me and others were applauding me for stepping up and that had me thinking about how many other men out there are suffering because they were violated as a child. I never thought about becoming an advocate for anything before but I felt this subject was something I needed to take on.

I went online and studied how to set up a podcast and then I purchased all of the equipment, now all I needed was a name for my podcast. I needed to take my time and come up with a name.

Meanwhile, I had to get to work, because tax season was approaching and I wouldn't have time for anything. I was so proud of myself because just a year ago I was fired from my job, in therapy, and I had no direction.

CHAPTER ELEVEN

WHAT DOESN'T KILL YOU MAKES YOU STRONGER

I got served with court papers, Sabian's mother Lorraine, and her husband Gill were out for my blood, my money, and my sanity. Two weeks before Thanksgiving I received papers from a lawyer, they were suing me for loss of life, defamation of character, and pain and suffering. I don't know where they think I get that kind of money from.

I had to put everything on hold to wrap my head around the calamity that was about to happen and to top everything off, Michael had ghosted me. After we came back from the Bahamas I've barely seen or talked to him. Every time I called him, it either went to voice mail or he answered and didn't have time to talk to me. I didn't know what was going on because I thought he was really into me. My thoughts were all over the place with him.

I couldn't focus on my business; I was missing client appointments and I accidentally gave one of my biggest client misinformation that caused him to get audited by the IRS and he was mad at me. My phone wasn't ringing off of the hook for accounting help and to top everything off Gary's child support stopped because he lost his job.

I would've said things could not get any worst but that would have been a lie, things did get worst.

Gary J came home for the Holiday break and I was happy to see him, I couldn't believe how different he looked even though it was only a few months since he left for college. I was glad to have him home despite my troubles.

It was a Tuesday afternoon; I was sitting in my office when Gary J walked in with mail in his hands.

"Ma, what's going on why aren't you paying the bills?"

At first, I wanted to leap at him because how dare he question me as if I owe him an explanation but then I thought, "Nope he's a man now I might as well be honest."

"Gary, I am having a little setback, but everything will be okay. I have some money in stocks and tax season is coming up."

"Ma, what's this I hear about my brother being molested, why didn't you tell me you were going to do an interview. Are you trying to ruin my life?"

Now I knew he was just like his selfish ass daddy, "Gary J everything is not about you. I needed to tell your brother's story."

"Why, he's dead, and nobody cares, but you!"

Before I knew it, I stood up and slapped the shit out of him, "Shut up, that's my son and I care, you are selfish just like your father and look where he's at nowhere. Your brother was who he was because of what happened to him!"

"Well, if you had been a better mother it wouldn't have happened, having a baby at fourteen was dumb."

It didn't process at first, so it took me a minute. I mean, I didn't hear what I thought I heard, and then it hit me. I lost it and started beating his ass and cursing him out. I didn't know if he was fighting back or not because I blanked out.

"How dare you say I was a bad mother after everything I put into this family, all the sacrifices I made so you, your brother, and sister could have. I gave you everything of me and things I never had. Look around you, this house, the clothes you wear, and the college you go to. I grew up hard, with no food, no water, no electricity, no clothes, no mother, and a crackhead for a father. I dreamed of the life I provided for all of you and yes I said I was because your father was along for the ride. So how dare you, nigga!"

When I finished I was out of breath and standing over him.

I burst into tears; he got up and ran out of the house and jump into his car to go God knows where and I didn't care.

That episode put me into a deep depression, I grabbed a bottle of rum from the bar, closed the blinds and crawled into bed with my clothes on, and laid there the entire day drinking until I fell asleep forgetting I needed to pick up Amanda from daycare.

My cell phone was ringing back-to-back, it woke me up, "Hello,"

It was Gary, "Shanna, you left our daughter in daycare!"

"Oh I'm sorry, I'll go and get her now."

"No, I have her and why did you put your hands on my son, he looks terrible! He said you beat him up for no reason!"

Gary was screaming on the phone, so I hung up on him, turned my phone off, and went back to sleep.

I had slept and drunk for three days; I didn't know day from night or night from day. It was Friday and I was still in bed. I couldn't get it together because my mind was spinning. The grief from the loss of my son's failed marriage, an ungrateful son, and a horrible childhood finally caught up with me. I didn't want my life anymore.

Who was looking for Shanna, who was going to rescue Shanna, who was going to make sure I was okay, no one. I couldn't ask Meeka or Reginald; they had their own lives to live. I couldn't talk to Michael; he threw me away just like everyone else I invested in. In my mind, I would be better off dead.

The day before Thanksgiving

I heard voices in the house so I jumped up and walked downstairs, I saw my ex-husband and my son raiding the refrigerator. "What is going on?" I startled both of them.

Gary walked over toward me, "We are getting some things for Thanksgiving dinner."

"Why aren't you at the grocery store, this is not an open market, put my shit back."

Gary J stopped and dropped everything.

I walked over to him, "You're not going to speak to me."

He leaned back, I could only imagine the smell that came roaring out of my mouth.

"No, you attacked me, what I look like speaking to you."

I raised my hand to smack him but his father caught my hand.

"Do not put your hands on him or I will have you locked up."

"Get off of me, and both of you get the hell out of my house!"

"You are pathetic, you look like shit and you smell like shit," says Gary.

"This coming from a motherfucker that ain't shit," I got in his face, "You know what you are, you are a sorry motherfucker and I hate the day I met you or had your children."

"Mommy, you don't want me?"

I turned around and saw my baby girl, my precious and innocent baby girl, "Yes, come here."

Gary stopped her, "No, she's staying with me, I'm filing for custody because clearly, you have lost your damn mind."

"Amanda come here come to me!"

She looked scared and I couldn't blame her, she didn't recognize me. I started crying.

"Let her go, Amanda come to mommy baby, I love you."

Gary picked her up and she clung to him with fear.

"What is going on, why is everyone turning against me? I'm not the bad person he is."

They walked toward the door, "Gary please, please don't take my children," I fell to the floor if there was any compassion in his heart for me, now was the time for him to show it.

He walked out of my home with my daughter in his arms and his arm around my son and just like that they rode off.

I stretched out on the floor crying and pounding the floor, asking why me God.

I wasn't festive.

The only reason I knew it was Thanksgiving Day was because of what I saw on TV. Yesterday's events played in my head over and over and I knew if I didn't get it together I was going to lose the one purpose in my life and that was being a mother. If I let Gary take my children I would essentially be doing what my mother did to me and my siblings and I didn't want to follow in her footsteps but I was lost.

I finally decided to take a shower, I let the hot water run down my braided hair onto my face and body, it felt so good; I stood in one place.

I stepped out of the shower, my body felt refreshed but my mind was cloudy. I put on a pair of leggings and a tank and looked around my room it was a mess. I shook my head but it was no need to make up the bed I planned to get right back in it.

I walked down to the kitchen, and the smell damn near knocked me out, the trash can needed to be emptied. I took the trash out, and my neighbor saw me and waved, I didn't wave back I didn't have the energy to speak.

I walked down to the mailbox, and something told me to check it, "Oh my goodness," it was full. I brought the mail in, "Bills, bills, bills, bills, bills, bills, wait what is this?"

I ripped it open; it was a check from the State of Maryland for fifty thousand dollars, I started jumping up and down. I forgot all about the lawsuit I had against the state for Wendell's death. I stared at the check and it was a reminder that my son was dead. I threw the check on the counter and went back upstairs to my bedroom and got back in bed. I hugged my pillow and cried; I wanted the pain from life to go away. I wasn't normal, never have been, and never will be because of other people fucking over my life.

I got served court papers again.

I guess my absence finally hit everyone; my mother called, my sister called and she never called unless she was in town, and my brother called me. I'm not going to lie; I was upset about not hearing from Michael.

I got a burst of energy from somewhere so I cleaned up the house, went through all of my mail, drove to the bank, and deposited the fifty thousand dollars. I was able to pay all of the house bills and have a cushion. I was back until I got served, yep Gary kept his word he was taking me to court for Amanda and asking for child support.

Bingo, that's what this is really about, but if he thinks for one second I'm going to let him have my baby he can think again because I was not going to let it happen anyway. I got on the phone, called my attorney, and explained what was going on. After talking to my attorney I knew I was in a fight for my life but for my baby, I was going to fight to the death.

I called Gary and didn't get an answer it went straight to voicemail; I knew he liked playing games so I got dressed and went to his apartment.

When I pulled up I didn't see his car or Gary J's car, where were they, after all, Gary didn't have a job to my knowledge. I walked up to the apartment and it looked empty, with no curtains or anything. I knocked on the door and there was no answer. "Where in the hell is my daughter!" Now I'm mad again.

I grabbed my phone and started calling his friends and family to get answers and I did when I spoke with his brother.

"Where is your brother he has Gary J and Amanda?"

His wife took the phone, "Hello, Shanna, this is Gail."

"Gail, what is going on?"

"Big Gary is locked up and the children are with us."

I heard Amanda in the background, "Can I speak to my mommy?"

"Put my daughter on the phone."

"Mommy can you come and get me, I' don't want to be here."

"I'm coming, put Gail back on the phone."

"Gail, what is your address," she gave me the address and I hopped into my car and hurried over there, I couldn't get there fast enough and it was evident because I heard the police as soon as I ran the light. "Dammit."

I looked through my rear-view mirror and saw Michael walking toward me wearing dark sunshades, my heart was pounding, and my hands started sweating and shaking.

He tapped on the window, and I rolled the window down.

"Hello, did you run the redlight because you have an emergency?"

I have never assaulted a police officer but this motherfucker is trying to play me. He acted as if he doesn't know me, as if he wasn't just eaten my ass a few months ago. "Okay, calm down Shanna."

"Yes as a matter of fact I do have an emergency."

"What is it?"

I turned to face him, and I was hoping the look on my face said, "Nigga really."

"My daughter is at her uncle's house and she shouldn't be there, she should be with her father but he's locked up."

"Okay," he tapped my car, "you can go."

Just like that, no "how have you been, happy holidays, sorry I haven't called," something, instead I got nothing. You know what fuck him and I pulled off. I wanted to cry but I was concerned too about Amanda to cry over his silly ass.

I pulled up at Gary's brother's house, and he met me at the door, "Gary told me not to let you have her."

"Lee I'm only going to say this once, get the fuck out of my way and give me my daughter. She has no business here with you."

His wife came out with Amanda along with her things, "Here she is Shanna, I don't know what's going on but I am not keeping a child away from her mother.”

“Thank you, Gail, at least somebody got some sense around here.”

Amanda jumped on me, and I almost fell. She laid her head on my shoulder, “I missed you. I don’t want to live with Daddy.”

“Don’t worry you don’t have to,” I looked up and Gary J was coming out of the house with his bags. “Where are you going?”

“Home with you.”

“Oh no, you are a grown man and you chose what side you were on, so since you think I’m a bad stupid mom, you stay right here where your father left you.”

“Ma no, please let me come home with you,” he was pleading.

I kept walking, and I didn’t feel bad.

He ran up behind me, “Ma, please, you gone leave me here?”

“Yes, I am, I’m tired of you not caring about anybody but you, I’m tired of fighting with you, you are not my man or my father you are my son, and since you can’t act like it, and since you have all of the answers you shouldn’t need me for anything.”

“Mommy, please.”

I looked at him and smiled, “No sir, that won’t work this time, and I will no longer be paying for your housing on campus or sending you money. You are nineteen and that means you are an adult.”

I put Amanda in the backseat of the car and drove off, I didn't bother to ask why Gary was in jail for now however it did mean getting custody just became a problem for him.

I looked at my baby sitting in the back sleeping so peacefully, and I knew I needed to get my shit together because I can't ever sink so low that I stop being her mother.

I was on a mission to be a better me.

Amanda and I decorated the house for Christmas, it was going to be me and her, and we were going to make the best out of it.

Gary called me several times from jail and I didn't answer the call, we didn't need to be bothered by him. Gary J left his uncle's house and went back to Howard. I didn't know how he was going to pay his rent for the upcoming year but that was a problem for him, not me. At least he had someplace to stay until December 31st.

I spent more money on Amanda for Christmas than I planned to but I wanted her to have an awesome Christmas.

The night before Christmas, I peeped into her room; she was on her knees praying, I stood by the door to listen.

"God, tell my brother Wendell I said hello, bless Gary J, I hope Santa brings him lots of stuff and he gets good grades in school, bless Mommy and Daddy. God please forgive Daddy for what he did and let him out so he can be with me and Mommy because we need him. God bless all the kids that don't have a mommy and daddy like me and give them all the presents. Good night God."

The innocence of children can break your heart. No matter how I felt about Gary she loved him.

I wanted to go to sleep but my mind was racing so I decided to go onto social media and see if I had any new messages regarding my interview and indeed I did. One, in particular, stood out to me, from a man "How do you tell your girl you were molested when you were a child, it's harder for men to tell their story than women."

Hmmm, I never thought about that. I really needed to work on a podcast but with tax season a few days away there was no way I could do that now.

I could never get used to setting up the toys by myself, Gary was the one putting the gifts around the tree but I had better get used to it because I was alone. As I was setting everything out my phone rang, it was one in the morning, who was this?

"Hello Gary J."

"Hi ma, I called to wish you a Merry Christmas and tell you I love you."

"I love you too, son," I was getting ready to hang up but he said something.

"I got a job and I applied for housing and got it. I'm sorry for everything I put you through and the things I said to you. I'm not saying this because I want to come home, I really mean it. I don't want to be like my dad, I love him too, but I saw the hurt he caused you and I saw what Wendell Jr put you through and you deserve better from me. I need to be the man you never had."

All I could say was "Wow," but I kept quiet and listened because it sounded good but I needed a show and tell not a say and no show.

"Ma are you there?"

"Yes, I'm here and I'm listening."

"That's all I got; tell Amanda I'll call her in the morning."

"Thank you for calling, and I appreciate you apologizing. I only want the best for you."

"I know and you deserve my best."

Well, I sure as hell wasn't expecting that but I'll take it.

Christmas Day.

I didn't get much sleep; I had to bake cookies and make sure Santa I mean me ate them.

Amanda got up early, I heard her run downstairs to see what Santa had gotten her. I could hear her screaming.

I went down to see her surprised face, 'Wow somebody has been good."

She had the biggest smile on her face, "Mommy look, look at all this stuff."

My cell phone rang, it was a face time call, I answered it and it was Gary wearing orange.

"Hey Shanna, is Amanda around?"

"Yes, but she's opening her gifts right now, she's busy."

"Can I please see her, I miss her."

"Yeah, I can tell," I said to myself. I let her see him, after all, she did pray to God for him but I wanted to be petty. I handed her the phone.

"Daddy," her eyes lit up brighter than the Christmas tree.

"Hey Mandy, Merry Christmas, what are you doing?"

"Opening my presents that mommy, I mean Santa Claus bought."

I looked over at her, it was about time she realized it.

"When are you coming home?"

"I don't know but it will be soon, I promise."

Here we go with the bullshit, he can't promise anything.

"Let me speak with your mother."

"Here Mommy he wants to talk to you." She handed me the phone.

I laid the phone down so he couldn't see my face.

"Shanna, I need a big favor, my girl got me a lawyer and he needs a letter from my ex-wife about my character can you write the letter?"

I started doing the hallelujah dance in the kitchen, "My footstool, Lord, you said you would make him my footstool."

"SHANNA, SHANNA!"

I couldn't stop.

"Yes, Lord, you said it," I picked up the phone, "let me get this straight, your freedom hinges on me writing a letter to the judge about your character. You need to ask somebody else to do it."

"Shana I know I have not been the best person to you but can you do it for our daughter."

"The daughter you wanted to take from me, while I was going through a tough time?"

"I helped you raise your son; he wasn't my child and I was a father to him."

"And so many more, isn't that right?"

"Shana, please, I need you."

"I'll think about it and let you know."

"Can I call my daughter back later today?"

"Sure, and you don't need to speak with me."

I hung up that phone and started humming, I put on some Christmas music, and Amanda and I sang Christmas carols.

After breakfast I cleaned up and started preparing dinner, there was a knock at the door, it was Meeka and her family. "Hey, come on in."

"We're the first ones here," asked Meeka.

"Who else is coming," did I forget something.

"Everybody, remember it's your Christmas to host the dinner."

Oh no, I forgot, thank goodness I cooked and stocked up on liquor, okay, make yourself at home.

Minutes later the doorbell rang it was my cousin Demy and his family and before long it was my aunts and cousins, my mother, and my sister; she came up from Florida. I had a house full of people and thank God they brought food.

I looked around and I felt the absence of my sons, it felt weird because I had a house full of guests but I still felt lonely. I felt sad inside.

I put on a smile for everyone. We played cards, I brought out the microphone and we sang. I wanted everyone to have a good time.

A New Year, A New Me

I brought in New Year's glued to my computer the taxes were coming in and even though the IRS wasn't taking returns yet that didn't stop the people from sending me their stuff.

Gary's court date was in January and he and his lawyer were calling me about the letter he needed. I wrote the letter but I was hesitant about giving it to the attorney.

He was calling Amanda every day when she got home from school, hoping he could talk to me, but I said no each time.

One night I got a call after office hours from an unknown number and I started not to answer it because Amanda and I were watching a movie together, it was her time.

"Hello, can I speak to Shanna?"

"Hi, this is Shanna, how can I help you."

"This is Belinda, Gary's girlfriend."

Oops, no she's not calling me, "Why are you calling me?"

"We are waiting for the letter, I paid for his lawyer and he needs the letter from you so Gary can get out of jail. If my lawyer doesn't get the letter Gary is looking at twenty-five years."

I sat up and looked around, somebody was pranking me, I was being punked. I started laughing, "Who is this, seriously?"

"What, this is Gary's girlfriend."

Her tone and her volume were wrong, this bitch was on eight and I was about to be on ten and then I looked over at Amanda and I thought "Why am I going to ten, they need me."

"Hello," she said.

"I'm still here, Belinda."

"Do you have the letter; I can come pick it up or you can email it to his attorney."

This bitch got balls for her man and clearly, he doesn't know she's making this call because he would have warned her but, nevertheless. "It seems like you have things under control from here." I hung up that phone and blocked her ass, he was her problem, not Shanna's problem anymore.

I went back to watching the movie with my baby.

That night I read the letter I had written and all of the wonderful things I said about Gary, he did have good qualities here and there. If he did twenty-five years my baby would be a grown woman with children when he came home.

I emailed the letter to his lawyer and went to bed.

"

CHAPTER TWELVE

MANIA

I wasn't getting any sleep and the night before court was worse for me. My mind was running and wasn't with numbers it was facing Sabian's parents in court. I ran every hypothetical there was in my head. I thought about what they would say and what I would say back to them. I couldn't turn the conversations in my head off.

I looked at the prescription Dr. Parker wrote for me I even googled what the effects and side effects were and I just could not bring myself to be on crazy medication. I felt that it would suppress my creativity and slow me down and my clients needed me to be creative as possible but I'm not going to lie, I needed the conversations in my head to stop immediately.

I don't know why I was so nervous; I hired a great attorney even though I felt I could represent myself. I wasn't a lawyer but I wasn't a dummy either, this was their day in court my day in court would soon follow.

I drove by Wendell's house to pick him up, he wanted to go to court with me and since he had been doing good with his sobriety I told him he could come along. His support was appreciated.

We walked into the courtroom together and I sat next to my attorney, Wendell sat behind me. I looked around the courtroom and memories of my son flashed into my head. It was so strong that I closed my eyes it was a jolt to my heart.

I heard the courtroom doors open so I turned around, it was Loraine and Gill. Loraine rolled her eyes at me but Gill looked straight ahead he didn't recognize his old friend Wendell sitting behind me. It's been many years since anyone has seen Wendell clean.

I watched as Loraine and Gill whispered to their attorney and there it was again the voices in my head talking to me.

When I looked over at Gill I was disgusted he was a pedophile, and a piece of shit that didn't deserve to live.

The judge walked in and I became nervous. The state's attorney read my charges. I was charged with defamation of character and they were suing me for the death of their son.

My patience was wearing off as they read the charges, I flickered my pen on the table as he talked. My attorney stopped me a few times but I couldn't help it.

My attorney said what needed to be said which was, Wendell was tried as an adult and therefore his mother and father cannot be sued.

Loraine and Gill weren't pleased and it showed all over their face but we weren't done, next was the defamation lawsuit.

The state's attorney asked me to approach the bench with my attorney. I thought that was odd, so I started tapping on the desk with my pen again.

"You are disgusting," said Loraine.

I ignored her, and it pissed her off.

"You, your son, and your family ain't shit. Your father was a crackhead and your mother was a drunk ass whore!"

Clearly, she wanted to battle however I was aiming for war, and therefore, I had nothing to say to her.

My lawyer walked back to the table and informed me that Gill did not want to proceed with the defamation of character.

That was okay by me but again I was waging a war.

Just as we were about to leave the courthouse I saw my surprise handed to Gill,. He was served papers charging him with molestation.

It gave me such pleasure to see the dreadful look on his face as he and his wife stood side by side but his look wasn't as pleasing as the look on her face when she looked at the man she married.

I wanted to scream, "Yes bitch you are married to a rapist" but I didn't.

Wendell walked toward Lorraine and Gill; I grabbed him but he yanked away from me. I don't know what Wendell said, but I saw the bitch in Gill come full circle.

Loraine pushed Wendell. "Get away from my husband, you junkie!"

I knew I had to get Wendell fast, "Come on we will have our day in court."

Wendell got up in Gill's face, "You and I were friends, man we got high together, and we ran the streets together. Your mother was his babysitter and you raped him; I should kill your ass right here!"

I had to calm Wendell down before he got locked up, but then I thought, "They got our son killed."

I saw the rage in Wendell, the street Wendell.

You put a hit out on our son to keep him quiet, you didn't want this shit to come out." Wendell stepped closer to Gill.

That nigga thought he saw a ghost, Wendell showed his gangsta side.

"I don't know what you're talking about. I did no such thing." Gill was stuttering.

I wanted to spit on Gill, "The police talked to the dude that stabbed him and he's talking, you paid for a hit because my son was getting ready to expose you. He wrote you a letter months before his stabbing didn't he."

I couldn't hold it in so I blurted it all out, "he told his counselor everything, about how you molested him when he was at your mother's house and he wasn't the only child you did this to. You molested the little girls too. I know everything Gill and so will everyone else."

The blood left Lorraine's, light skin, she looked pale in the face.

Loraine walked away and Gill followed behind her out of the courthouse and they weren't holding hands like they were entering the courthouse.

Wendell looked at me, "I'm going to kill him, Shanna."

I acted like I didn't hear him.

The next few weeks were a blur, I couldn't focus and my thoughts were all over the place even though tax season was over.

Gary was out of jail and spending quality time with Amanda, he took her to DC for the weekend to see Gary J. I had the weekend to myself and I was not going to sit around the house and Meeka made sure of that.

Saturday night, it was humid as hell in Delaware, A group of us decided to go skating. I hadn't skated in years, the last time I went skating was with Gary, Wendell, and Gary J; Amanda wasn't born yet. I went anyway.

I showed up looking cute with my jeans, and t-shirt on, and my hair pulled up into a ponytail; I looked young. I needed something to get my mind off of everything going on in my life.

We walked into the skating rink and it was packed. I put on my skates and hit the floor, literally. Damn, I was rusty, but I got up and skated around and I was doing pretty good for an old lady.

Meeka skated over to me, "Is that Michael over there at the door?"

I looked over there and my heart sank down to my stomach, yes it was Michael. I swear to God he is the only black cop in Delaware, he is everywhere. I tried to ignore him but my eyes kept going over there to where he was. Depression hit me, I started feeling rejected and I got quiet. Meeka noticed right away, that's a best friend for you.

"Go over there and say something to him."

"No he ghosted me; I'm not going to say anything to him."

Meeka stood up, "If you don't I will."

I knew she was serious, "No, don't do that, that's embarrassing."

"No, what's embarrassing is my best friend being a chump."

"Excuse me,"

Meeka and I looked at the stranger. "Yes," says Meeka.

"Are you here alone," he looked right at me.

"I am, why" I was suspicious he could have been someone Gill sent to kill me.

"I want to skate with you."

"Who are you and what is your name, you don't just walk up here and asked to skate with someone without introducing yourself," Meeka didn't hold back.

'I'm sorry," he laughed, "Your right, my name is Alfred, I'm here with my daughter, she's right over there."

"Okay sure, "I skated out on the floor with him, they were playing a slow song. I looked over at Michael to see if he was looking and he wasn't.

Alfred, hmmm; he was tall and attractive. I wonder why did he single me out to skate with, it's packed in here with women but he chose me? There I go again, thinking too much.

"I didn't get your name."

"My name is Shanna."

"Are you dating anyone?"

I looked up at him, "Don't you think that's extra?"

"No, I want to know. I don't want some muscle man to come in here and say, "Get off of my woman."

We both laughed.

"You are funny, no you don't have to worry about that happening, I'm single."

"For now," he murmured.

"What did you just say?"

"I said for now."

He sure was confident, I just wished that I was.

The song ended and I pulled away from him to leave the floor.

"Can I have your phone number?"

I hesitated before answering, "Sure, why not." I gave him my number.

"I'm going to call you and you'll have my number."

His daughter skated over to us, "Dad, can I get a pizza."

"Don't be rude, say excuse me."

I was impressed by that, "hi I'm Shanna."

"Hi, I'm Alexis."

"Nice to meet you, Alexis, "I shook her hand."

"Dad, can I get the pizza?"

He handed her some money and I walked away.

"Shanna, Shanna, would you like something to eat?"

"No, I'm good but thank you."

I looked over at Michael again and I couldn't tell if he was looking at me or not because he had sunglasses on. I wanted to say something to him so bad.

We left the skating rink around ten and I had to drive forty-five minutes home. I was tired, my legs were sore and I felt sleepy. I turned the music on to help me stay woke.

I was ten minutes away from home when my cell phone rang and it was Alfred.

"Hello,"

"Hi Shanna, I was calling to see if you got home safe."

'I'm about ten minutes away."

"Call me, when you get settled."

"Okay, I will." We hung up and I started thinking, who is this dude and why is he coming on so strong."

I parked my car in the driveway and started in the house when Gary pulled up with Amanda. I knew he could not do a full weekend and no doubt a bitch was involved.

Gary walked me to the door, "Hey, she wanted to come home."

"This late, why not tomorrow?"

"She kept saying I want Mommy."

I opened the door, "Go up to your room and I'll be up in a minute."

"I never got an opportunity to thank you for writing the letter on my behalf."

I didn't do it for you, I did it for your children, they love you even though I don't."

"You don't love me."

"No Gary, why is that surprising."

"Because I love you, no matter what we go through I will always love you."

"You mean no matter what you put me through."

"Shanna," he touched my arm.

"Don't touch me please."

"Shanna, I have never loved or had a love for any other woman besides you and I never will. I know I wasn't the best husband or father but I did the best that I had knowledge of. You learn where you live."

I was not about to listen to the bullshit, "Gary goodnight." I tried to close the door but he stop me, was he crazy.

"Wait, I want to tell you something about Wendell Jr."

He had my full attention, "What."

"I did think something was off about his behavior, after Gary J was born he became obsessed with his brother, he didn't want me to touch him when you weren't home. When we had a man-to-man talk about sex he did not want to discuss sex at all."

Now he tells me, I needed to know back then, "Okay thanks," I closed the door and walked upstairs. I looked into Amanda's room and she was knocked out of sleep.

I couldn't stop yarning, I took a shower and jumped into my bed, and as soon as I fell asleep my phone rang. "hello" I answered.

"Hey, it's me, Alfred."

"Oh, I forgot to call you, I'm home safely and in my bed."

"So tell me about yourself."

Was this man deaf, I told him I was in the bed. "Alfred I am sleepy."

"Okay, I'll call you tomorrow, sleep well."

I hung up the phone, now I can't get back to sleep I should call his ass and wake him up at two a.m.

Instead, I laid in bed and thought and thought and thought some more. I couldn't shut it off.

Summertime,

Gary J wanted to come home for the summer and get a job; I missed him so I let him but I laid down some rules, no girls in his room, and he had a curfew. He was twenty but in my house, there was a curfew at my door.

Conversations with Alfred were good, he was entertaining but I didn't want to get serious and I wasn't ready to go out with him or share any details of my life. I wanted to take it slow because Michael taught me a lesson.

I couldn't wrap my head around why he paid for an expensive trip and then dumped me. It didn't make sense to me.

My attention span was short leading up to the court date. I would think about what was going to happen and then how I was going to respond to something that didn't even happen. I felt myself getting depressed. I was thinking about my childhood, about my father, my mother, and my lack of a relationship with my siblings and I was going nowhere fast. If I wasn't working and crunching numbers to distract me I would have a million things running through my head.

The last straw was when I was driving home from the grocery store, it was raining hard and I could barely see in front of me. Amanda was in the back seat and Gary J was in the passenger seat. My mind drifted and I started thinking about Gill molesting my son, and my thoughts carried away and I forgot I was driving and ran the red light.

I heard Amanda scream and Gary J yelled, "Ma lookout," but it was too late, we were hit. A car ran into my driver's side and flipped my BMW car over and the airbags deployed.

"Oh my God, Amanda, Gary J!" I was yelling for them but I didn't hear them. I started screaming for help.

I heard people around me talking but I couldn't make out what they were saying. I could see Gary J but I could not see Amanda. I became hysterical and I started crying I didn't want to lose my babies. I heard the sirens getting closer.

When I opened my eyes and looked around I was in the emergency room at Christiana Care Medical Center, I screamed, "Where are my children!"

I jumped off the bed, I was sore, and my arm was bruised. I ran into the hallway right into a doctor, "Where is my son and my daughter!"

The doctor tried to calm me, but I needed to know where my children were, "I'm not going to calm down until I see my children dammit!"

I looked past the doctor and saw Gary, "Gary, where are my kids!"

Gary ran down the hall to me, I fell into his arms, "Where are my children, Gary?"

"Gary J is fine but, but …….."

"But what, what!"

"Amanda is in intensive care; she didn't have her car seat on so she got banged up pretty bad."

I screamed that's all I could do." "Take me to her now."

"Ms. Cole, you have to go back into the room so we can treat you!"

"Fuck you, I want to see my children, Gary take me to my children right now or I am going to flip everything in here over and you know I will!"

"Okay, okay, I'll take you to them if you promise to let the doctor check you out," Gary spoke calmly.

I stared into his eyes, while my heart was racing, "Okay, okay but promise me you will stay with her until I get out of here."

"I promise you; I will stay with her; she's going to be fine."

I walked back into the room; the doctor was probing my body and asking me questions but I couldn't hear him because the voices in my head were louder. "Turn them off!"

"Ms. Cole, what is wrong, turn who off?"

I looked at the doctor, "There are voices in my head, please, please turn them off."

"Ms. Cole, are you taking any medication for mental health?"

"No, I'm not crazy, I'm not crazy!"

I had to calm down so I started taking deep breaths, "Oh God, make it stopppppppp," I screamed inside my head.

Hours later the doctors discharged me and Gary J and neither one of us heard from Gary about Amanda. I ran through the hospital to intensive care, when I got there Gary's family was sitting in the waiting area. I tried to prepare myself for the worst when I opened the door, but I knew nothing could prepare me to see my baby laying in a hospital bed.

The nurse took me into the room and when I saw her hooked up to machines and her precious eyes closed I broke down into tears, "Oh no, my baby," I kneeled next to her bed and prayed, "God, don't take another child from me, please spare her life."

Days turned into nights and my baby still wasn't coming around, but I wasn't giving up. My family, friends, and I prayed around the clock.

One week after the accident Amanda had improved but she wasn't out of the woods just yet. However, the doctors were hopeful.

Gary never left my side; he was torn just as I was and I know he wanted to blame me but he kept it to himself.

Prayers answered.

Amanda was in the hospital for a month and a half before we could bring her home and the doctor said she would make a full recovery.

Her father didn't waste any time blaming me for the accident, he went in on me and the things he said hit me hard. I went into a deep depression; I didn't want to get out of bed.

I called my mother and asked her to come over and help me with Amanda, I hadn't asked for her help in years and but I needed her because mentally I had checked out.

Day after day I lay in bed, blinds, and curtains closed, and I turned off all communication with everyone.

Amanda would knock on my bedroom door and call my name but I didn't answer. I was at my lowest, I wanted to die. What was I living for, I failed all of my children and I felt they would be better off without me.

One morning I heard the birds chirping, they were loud, I got up and peeped out the blinds; the morning sun hit my eyes it was blinding; I put my hand up to block it. When I lifted my arm the funk from my body nearly knocked me out, "I stink."

There was a knock at my bedroom door, I looked at the bottom of the door and I could tell it was Amanda. "Mommy, good morning."

I opened the door; I couldn't ignore my baby any longer. I forced a smile on my face, and opened the door, "Good morning, beautiful,"

She grabbed me around my waist and hugged me tight. I burst into tears.

"Mommy we love you, it's not your fault, we are okay, God saved us."

God bless my baby; she knew just what to say.

I wanted to pick her up but she was too big and my body was still sore from the car accident I grabbed her hand, "Come on and get in my bed with me." We hoped into my bed and then Gary J knocked on the door, "hey ma,"

I was surprised to see him, I thought he had left for college.

"Hey come on and get in my bed, let's lay here and talk."

Gary J climb on top of my bed too, "Hey ma,"

"Yes,"

"I love you; I know I haven't been the best son, but I don't want anything to happen to you," he started crying.

"Come here," I hugged him, "I love you too and we are going to be okay, I promise."

"Mommy, Mr. Michael came here to check on you, he left you some really pretty flowers, and he had some for me too."

"Yeah ma, he was cool," said Gary J

"I'll call him later, right now I just want to enjoy my babies," I started tickling Amanda and we laughed, I felt good.

I was ready to get back to my life. I smelled food so I walked downstairs, I couldn't believe my eyes, there were roses everywhere. "Oh my God where did these roses come from?" All of them had a card, I read one of the cards, "Get well soon beautiful, signed Michael."

My mom was in the kitchen cooking, "Well look who is out of bed."

My mother walked up to me and hugged me, "I was worried about you."

I didn't know how to respond, I hugged her back but it felt odd. I could feel her crying.

"It's okay, I'm good," I broke the hug "but these flowers, Michael sent all of these?"

"Yes, he did," he's a nice guy.

I was confused, he has ghosted me for almost a year and he sends me flowers because I was in an accident. This was weird.

My cell phone rang, it was Alfred, "Hello, Alfred."

"Hey stranger, did I say or do something wrong to offend you?"

"No, not at all, I was in a car accident and I needed to take some time for myself."

"Are you okay?"

"Yes I am, we will talk but right now I am in the middle of something."

I couldn't believe the flowers I had to call Michael.

Before I could finish dialing the doorbell rang, "Shanna, Michael is at the door!"

I can't get in my head, "Be cool, Shanna."

Michael walked into the living room, "Hello Shanna, can we talk?"

"I'm going to leave and give you two some privacy, Shanna are you good."

"Yes, ma'am I am good."

He wasn't wearing his police uniform and he looked good, sexy good and I was wearing a bonnet and looked a mess "Have a seat."

"I know you think I'm crazy and I am, I I I I I I have some issues and it has cost me relationships and friendships. I walked away from you and I was wrong and I'm sorry. When I heard you on YouTube about your son being molested I didn't know how to proceed with us."

I was confused, "why, how did that affect us?"

"Let me explain."

He looked nervous and he started sweating.

"Do you know Gill, are you two related?"

"No, no, nothing like that."

"Well what, because you had me thinking I did something wrong."

"I was molested when I was a young boy," he burst out.

"Oh no, I'm so sorry, I'm so sorry."

"I don't want you to be sorry, you didn't do anything wrong. It's just that I heard you talking, I heard your pain and I just froze."

"But how could you be so cold, you pulled me over and you didn't say anything, you saw me at the skating rink, I know you did and you ignored me why now."

"Because I was there at the car accident, I saw you and the kids and I thought you weren't going to make it and I didn't want something to happen to you and I never told you why I stopped talking to you."

I stood up and paced the floor, "I thought it was me, you let me think it was me."

"I was wrong for that and I'm sorry."

"Damn right you were wrong, I liked you, I thought you were the one. I have gone through some shit with men and I had an ounce of faith in you mainly because you were a cop and I thought you had some integrity.

"I do have integrity but I have flaws also and just like your son, this shit is tough to deal with day in and day out. I am a grown-ass man and I still feel fucked up. These thoughts don't go away you learn how to cope and I didn't know how you would feel about me. Women think oh he's gay, he's crazy and I like you too much to have you lose respect for me."

I calmed down, "Okay, I'm still mad but I get it. Why did you send me all of these flowers?"

"I wanted you to have them, I care deeply about you and I don't want to hurt you."

What did he mean by hurting me, he confused me with that.

"Hurt me how?"

"That's a story for another day. I just wanted to drop by and check on you."

"See there you go being evasive, we can't be friends like that because that shit confuses me and I don't need confusion." I had to be straight up with his ass.

"You deserve more, you're right but I'm not ready and just know it's me, not you."

"Okay," that's all I could really say.

We stood up and he held me, I melted into his body once again. I needed to pull back or I was going to take him upstairs and fuck him.

He left and I took a deep breath, I knew what my next move was, I had some decisions to make, "hello, my name is Shanna Cole and I would like to make an appointment."

CHAPTER THIRTEEN

HELP ME, PLEASE!

Ten months later.

I wanted my day in court with Gill but circumstances arose and that day never came because Karma has a way of taking care of things. I called it Karma but others called it a misfortunate thing that happened to a good man.

Good man my ass, he got what he deserved; two days before Halloween he was allegedly robbed, and when he refused to give up the money the gunman shot and killed him.

It's been two months and they still haven't caught the shooter.

Whoever they were, they saved me the trouble of having to use my black steel beauty and for that I thank them.

The streets were talking though, Wendell Sr disappeared into thin air like Houdini. I was told he moved to South Carolina with his cousins and is doing well for himself.

I pray that he stays clean and if my suspicions are right, well let's just say, Wendell did what his spirit led him to do.

I tried things my way and it was an epic fail. When I look back over my life I should have been here and I am so sorry it took me so long. I was trying to be strong because that's what I thought black women had to do. I was raised in a culture where we don't ask for help we are the help, helper, and helpmate but I can't live out the rest of my life under that umbrella.

The Pastor said to pray, it will work out; I prayed and fasted and my mind tricked me into believing that everything was alright.

What the Pastors needed to tell the congregation is, mental health is real and it can kill you if you don't get help.

People run to the doctor for high blood pressure and diabetes but no one is running to the doctor for their mental health.

I was living in fear of my own pain, not wanting to talk about it or acknowledge it because if I did it meant I was flawed.

I hid my mental suffering and the sad part is I didn't make myself this way, it was inflicted onto me. The people responsible never took responsibility they just watched me spiral out of control and then judged me and used me.

I have been looking for love, acceptance, and validation in every man that has come into my life since the day my father took his first hit of crack.

I worked my ass off to be a good mother, who was supposed to teach me, my mother? No, she was too busy living her best life.

I was living on my own at seventeen, I should have been going to my prom and enjoying being a teenager but I didn't have that luxury.

This is the icing on the cake I married my dad, I married a narcissistic jackass just like my dad. I didn't have sense enough to know that he was not the one because I was broken and I thought this man could make me whole.

And the two people who fucked me up don't want to talk about what they did to my life and I know why, they don't want to be reminded of the shit they did but guess who thinks about it every motherfucking day, ME!

There's not a day that goes by that I don't think about the drugs, the ass beatings, no food, being teased in school, no water no electricity and the list goes on.

It's not fair that they get a pass from me. I shouldn't be sitting in therapy alone, those motherfuckers need to be sitting here next to me, apologizing, and asking me for forgiveness.

Not one time did I ever stop to think I could be doing everything all wrong, I never hugged my children, but I provided. I never told them I loved them, but I provided for them.

I didn't give them what I wanted because I didn't know how.

God knows when I think about the past forty years of my life I cringe because I didn't have to hit rock bottom if someone would have just loved me enough to say, "Get some help" But no one is going to say that because we're black, and we're proud.

Fuck that! Fuck that!

How can we be black and proud and mentally drained and damaged?

Have you ever heard anyone say "She's a strong white woman; no, and you never will, and do you know why, ain't nothing strong about white? It's pure and angelic, but black is tough and strong and it's beautiful but no one ever looks at us as beautiful.

I am going to do whatever it takes to make sure my children get into therapy because I don't want Gary J and Amanda to waste years trying to figure stuff out on their own.

"Well, it seems that you are ready to embrace your mental health journey and you look great. Married life looks good on you.

I couldn't stop smiling, "yes the second time is a charm, married life is great."

There is something else you need to do, that will be a big help to your mental health."

"What is it, I'm ready."

"You need to forgive the people that hurt you."

"Why, what does that have to do with my mental health? I know what the bible says about forgiveness but God didn't go through what I did."

Dr. Parker laughed, "Yes you're right, he just had nails in his hands, thorns on his head, whipped, double-crossed by friends, and hung; I guess your ordeal was worse."

No doubt my therapist had a talent for sarcasm.

"The inability to forgive affects your psychosis and hinders our ability to move forward, therefore, keeping the brain trapped in pain."

I looked down at the floor and shook my head, "They need to ask me for forgiveness not me just say, "Hey, by the way, I forgive you for fucking up my life."

"Nope, not like that, do this; write each one a letter and express how you feel because of their actions toward you. Mail it and let it go and if they call you or reach out to you, you and that person can address it."

"Dr. Parker, you got me doing all the work for people that I don't even care about."

"You care, that's why you are where you are; it's time to heal."

She was right I was being dramatic as usual.

"Shanna, I don't typically do this," she stood up, "I want to give you a hug."

We hugged, it was awkward, it's amazing how growing up without physical love can impact a person's life.

"I'll see you in two weeks and tell your husband I said hello."

"Yes, I'll be back in two weeks and I'll be sure to tell him you said hello." I left Dr. Parker's office with a new perspective on my life and for the first time, I left with a smile.

On the way home I started thinking about what I would say in the letters and I couldn't get past "hello." I didn't know what to say that would heal me and not hurt them.

My Babe is calling, "Hello babe."

"Hey beautiful, are you on your way home?"

"I am, what would you like to eat tonight?"

"Don't worry about that, me and the kids cooked your favorite; I'll see you when you get here, and drive safe. I love you, Shanna."

"I love you too and I have a surprise."

"What, what is it."

"Calm down, I'll be there shortly.

I turned up my music, opened my sunroof, and enjoyed the sun before it set.

I pulled into the driveway, waved at our new neighbors, and made my way into the house. I was home and eager to get into the house and see my beautiful family. They say the second time is the best.

As usual, we had great conversations at the dinner table and he was attentive to what I had to say with no criticism.

One thing I learned about my mental health was I don't have to hide it from the people that love me and I can include them on my journey.

It was safe to love and that's all I ever wanted.

I finally got around to writing my letters and I kept them short, but before I wrote the letters I did the work to forgive them. I own no part of what was inflicted on me because none of that was my fault.

I did, however, look past my parents and into their lives and the bottom line is they were victims of circumstances just as I was.

Dear Mom,

I needed you and you were not there; I thought long and hard about why you abandoned us. But that's not my cross to bear.

My childhood was terrible and I spent years trying to get what I never got from you. I don't remember sitting between your legs getting my hair done or going shopping at the mall with you. I had to raise myself and it wasn't easy.

The great takeaway from my childhood was my love for children. I will never turn a blind eye to any child in need because I know what it felt like when people saw me starving, stinking, and unkept and they looked the other way.

I will be a refuge for children.

I forgive you and I release all anger that I have carried in my heart for you.

I love you and wish you the best.
Love Shanna

Dear Dad,

I looked up to you, you were my everything when I was a little girl. You could do no wrong until everything went terribly wrong. I don't know what your life was like when you were a child. If it was bad, I'm sorry you had to go through that and if it was good well I wish I could say the same.

The life you have provided for your new family is far greater than what you gave me and my siblings but at the end of the day, you have to live with that. You can pretend that it doesn't bother you but I am sure it does.

I started going to therapy and one of the things my therapist said is that I have to forgive the people that injured me. You and my mom are at the top of the list. You may think you don't need my forgiveness but I need to forgive you so I can live a better life.

So with that being said, I am in a better place and I can forgive you. I hope one day you can forgive yourself. I don't have a hell to put you in and I am not responsible for you going to heaven or hell.

I don't believe people die and go to hell I believe hell is on earth.

Shanna

Dear Wendell

Son, I dropped the ball and I hope you can forgive me. I am asking for forgiveness. I was too busy trying to give you that I didn't notice you.

I wasn't mentally able to love you because I wasn't right.

An evil person took your innocence and I am sorry that happened on my watch I was supposed to protect you, son. I prayed for your life and I hope your spirit is at rest.

I love you, son.

Dear Gary Sr.

I want to start off by saying I forgive you. I cannot hold on to the dislike that I feel for you. I have been angry with you since you cheated on me and truth be told I should have left you and not because of infidelity but because I didn't stay with you for the right reasons. I have never been in love with you ever. I loved you but never in love and you may have thought I was in love because of all the things I tolerated and excused in our marriage but no. I didn't know any better, I didn't love myself or trust myself enough to walk away and stay away. thank you for our two beautiful children, which was the best thing that came from our marriage for me.

I don't know what your future holds but I hope for the sake of our children that you put forth an effort to be great.

Shanna

Dear Shanna

You made a lot of mistakes but I can't blame you, your life had a lot of hick-ups in it. Actually, I'm surprised you're not sitting in a mental institution or in prison for killing the people who mishandled you. Thank you for working so hard to be the odds that were stacked against you.

I'm proud of you for getting to a place where you are reaching out for help because that has always been your downfall.

You never allowed people to help you, your pride and ego were too big to let people who truly love you shower you with love.

I know you never wanted to be indebted to anyone and standing on your own was important.

I forgive you for staying with Gary Sr longer than you needed to. I get it you wanted love but a piece of bread is not better than a loaf if you can't get full. You deserve the entire loaf.

Your love comes in many variations and sometimes baby girl you just need to tell people you love them.

Take care of Shanna first and you will see everything fall into place.

Who Did Shanna Marry?

Gary (re-marry)

Alfred

Michael

Shanna and Michael didn't go out on a date again and it didn't have anything to do with issues. She thought he was a great person but he wasn't the man for her and she wasn't going to settle again. They remained cordial to each other in passing.

Gary would always be Amanda and Gary J's father but that didn't mean he had to be her husband again. She wrote him a letter also forgiving him for the hurt he had put on her and through her healing she realized he was a product of his environment. It is said, hurt people hurt people and a narcissist will be a narcissist for life.

It didn't take Alfred long to show Shanna what he was made of, and of course, he wasn't perfect but that's not what she was looking for. Shanna wanted a man that saw her for who she was, her pain, her love, and her ability to produce.

Alfred didn't win her over with flowers, and gifts; he brought a piece of peace.

They had a modest wedding with Amanda, Gary J, and his daughter Alexis in Jamaica with a few family members and friends.

The End

A Word from the Author

Hello, I am Antoinette R. Davis and I hope you enjoyed my latest novel Lingering Effect if you did I would love to hear from you in your reviews or you can email me at Antoinettewrites@aol.com.

Writing is a passion of mine and I love to dive deep into issues that plague African American people and as hard as it is to talk about it is even harder to write about. However, the stories must be told and I want to tell them.

I talk to a therapist and I am not ashamed. I write these stories because I want my culture to remove the stigma of being ashamed of their mental health. It's hard in this world for African Americans and we should not be afraid or ashamed to seek help. With that being said don't waste your life trying to cope with situations when there are resources available for you.

I love you and I'll see you in my next book.

If you enjoyed this book and would like to read my other novels please go to www.1fictionqueen.com